An Historical Atlas of Modern Europe From 1789-1914,
With an Historical and Explanatory Text

AN HISTORICAL ATLAS
OF
MODERN EUROPE

FROM 1789 TO 1914

WITH AN HISTORICAL AND EXPLANATORY TEXT

BY

C. GRANT ROBERTSON, M.A., C.V.O.

FELLOW OF ALL SOULS COLLEGE OXFORD

AND

J. G. BARTHOLOMEW, F.R.S.E., F.R.G.S.

OXFORD UNIVERSITY PRESS
HUMPHREY MILFORD
LONDON   EDINBURGII   GLASGOW   NEW YORK   TORONTO
MELBOURNE   BOMBAY
1915

PRINTED IN ENGLAND
AT THE OXFORD UNIVERSITY PRESS

TABLE OF CONTENTS

LIST OF PLATES

INTRODUCTION

During the last few years there has been a marked increase in the study of the evolution of the State-system of modern Europe from the French Revolution to the present day. This increased study has not been confined to the English-speaking universities and schools on both sides of the Atlantic and in the great British colonies and dependencies. All citizens desiring to take an active and beneficial part in politics have felt the necessity of acquiring an accurate knowledge of the political history and conditions which have made the Europe of to-day, and which are the essential preliminary to any intelligent interpretation of ' foreign affairs' and of the motive forces, ambitions, and ideals governing the policy, diplomacy, and international relations of the European States.

The chief obstacle to such an indispensable study, whether in a university, a school, a trades-union, a political organization, or the home, has been the absence of adequate maps—the difficulty of finding an atlas providing the necessary guidance, illustration, and information—an atlas, of a reasonable compass and easily handled, with Plates on a sufficiently large scale, with the necessary explanatory text, and, above all, at a price within the means of the slenderest purse. Historical text-books written by first-rate scholars (I need only refer to the well-known works by Seignobos, Alison Phillips, Andrews, Hazen, Bourgeois, Débidour, and many others) there are in plenty. The standard historical atlases by Spruner-Menke, Droysen, Lablache, Schrader, and that issued under Mr. Poole's editorship by the Clarendon Press, are elaborate and scientific, but are necessarily very expensive, and cumbrous to handle ; like the school historical atlases, they contain a great deal more than what the student of modern Europe needs, and too often they fail to supply on the scale required just what is necessary. They do not, for example, deal with the most recent developments, and they leave a gap between their Plates and those of a purely modern atlas.

The outbreak of the Great War in 1914 has immensely stimulated the study of modern European history. To-day all over the world, in every quarter, questions are being asked which can only be adequately answered (if at all) with the help of the requisite historical maps. Furthermore, whatever may be the military result of the War, the governments and peoples of the European States are confronted with a European resettlement at some future date on a vaster scale, and involving vaster and more complicated issues than were handled even at the Congress of Vienna in 1814. The War and the settlement, it is practically certain, will give a further stimulus to the study of the European history of the nineteenth century, which properly begins with the French Revolution in 1789. The need, then, for an historical atlas on an adequate scale and at the lowest possible price is to-day urgent, and its urgency will increase. The present atlas has been planned to satisfy this need.

A brief explanation of its main features will indicate clearly the authors' interpretation of the requirements of students of all classes—for every intelligent citizen is in their eyes a student in the school of life and of politics—and of their methods for satisfying those needs. The atlas contains 29 full coloured Plates on an adequate scale and 14 half-Plates—43 maps in all. The historical starting-point in each case has been, broadly, the year 1789. But in several Plates—notably those of France (VII), Germany (XI), Austria (XIX), Poland (XXVII), and Russia (XXIX)—the map expressly includes material explanatory of the history and evolution of the State in question prior to 1789. Modern historical geography is not, and never can be, simply an affair of shifting political boundaries. The density and distribution of population, physiographical, ethnological, economic factors are of vital importance. The student will therefore find in Plates I-IV and in Plate XVIII cartographical representations of these. Each of the leading European States, commencing with France, is taken in order and its political and historical evolution carefully indicated and illustrated in a series of maps. Special attention has also been given to definable areas—the Mediterranean, the Baltic Lands, the Balkans—in which an examination of the area as a whole as well as of its component parts is essential to adequate knowledge. The development and interests of the European States outside the purely European area have been linked up by a series of special Plates with the purely European maps. The student, for example, will find Plates illustrating the expansion of Russia in the East, the Ottoman Empire in Asia, Persia, and the Persian Gulf, the political settlement of Africa, the distribution of power in the Far East and the colonies of the European States all over the world. In these, as in the purely European Plates, while 1789 has been taken as the starting-point, the political conditions prevailing on August 4, 1914, have always been the terminus. The atlas is, in a word, therefore a modern as well as an historical atlas, and has been planned to provide every kind of student with the material for understanding the Europe of the past and the present and for forecasting the Europe of the future. In the drawing and execution of the Plates care has been taken to employ an adequate scale and clear colouring, to ensure as high a degree of accuracy as is possible, and not to crowd the maps with irrelevant and confusing detail. The authors have, where necessary, deliberately subordinated detail to clearness and broad effects. But the scale on which the maps are drawn has enabled much valuable detail to be included without confusing or blurring the specific object of each separate Plate.

The Plates are prefaced by an explanatory historical text and commentary. In this the writer has endeavoured to include what is essential to the understanding of the map and the submerged history that it represents. Considerations of space and the cost of production have forbidden the attempt, foolish in any case, to provide a substitute for a first-rate historical text-book. No atlas, on however lavish a scale, can take the place of the standard historical works ; but without an adequate atlas those works are unprofitable and misleading. The object of this atlas is to provide what is indispensable; to convey and to illustrate what historical geography really means, and to prepare all who have the money, time, knowledge, and will to learn for more advanced study on the great and expensive works of reference, both atlases and histories.

Lastly, no attempt has been made to illustrate in detail the historical evolution of the British Empire, except in so far as it necessarily enters into the various Plates (e. g. Nos. V, VI, XXV, XXXIII, XXXIV, XXXV, XXXVI). There are three reasons for this. First, adequate treatment would have involved the addition of so many more Plates and printed matter as to increase very disadvantageously the price of the atlas and thereby destroy a feature of capital importance in the authors' eyes—a European historical atlas at the lowest possible price; secondly, *The Historical and Modern Atlas of the British Empire* (Messrs. Methuen & Co.), by the authors of the present atlas, provides at a moderate price, and on a much more liberal scale than could have been included in the present work, all the material necessary. The

two atlases are therefore complementary to each other. Thirdly, the crying need to-day is for an adequate historical atlas of the States of the Continent of Europe.

It is the intention of the authors, when the coming European settlement has been definitely concluded, to add all the Plates necessary to embody the full terms of that settlement, and thereby to retain and amplify the feature to which they attach the highest importance—the combination of an historical with a modern atlas.

The authors venture to claim that the present work provides a combination of features and material not to be found in, and at a price far lower than that of, any other historical atlas of which they have knowledge. It would not have been possible to produce at this price without the effective co-operation of the Oxford University Press. The author of the scheme, of the text, and of the material embodied in the Plates, expresses, therefore, to the University Press, and to his expert collaborator, Mr. Bartholomew, his grateful thanks.

ALL SOULS COLLEGE,
   OXFORD.

G. G. R.

BIBLIOGRAPHY OF HISTORICAL AND GEOGRAPHICAL WORKS

[NOTE.—This is not a complete or scientific bibliography, but simply a list of some of the important and helpful works of reference for advanced or special study.]

ATLASES

Historical Atlas of Modern Europe. Ed. R. L. Poole. Oxford : The Clarendon Press. (With explanatory text in English.)

VIDAL DE LA BLACHE. *Atlas général historique et géographique.*

F. SCHRADER. *Atlas de Géographie historique.* Paris, 1896. (With explanatory text in French.)

SPRUNER-MENKE. *Histor.-geograph. Hand-Atlas.* 3rd ed. 1880.

G. DROYSEN. *Allgemeiner histor. Hand-Atlas.* 1886.
(The explanatory text of both these atlases is in German.)

The Cambridge Modern History Atlas. With explanatory text in English. [Plates to illustrate the Camb. Mod. History.]

H. B. GEORGE. *The Relations of Geography and History.*

E. A. FREEMAN. *The Historical Geography of Europe, with Atlas.* 2 vols. 3rd ed. Ed. J. B. Bury.

A. HIMLY. *Histoire de la formation territoriale des États de l'Europe centrale.* 2 vols. [Very valuable and illuminating.]

J. PARTSCH. *Central Europe.* [Series—The Regions of the World.]

H. J. MACKINDER. *Britain and the British Seas.*

D. G. HOGARTH. *The Nearer East.* [Indispensable for the Balkan area.]

A. LITTLE. *The Farther East.*

J. S. KELTIE. *The Partition of Africa.* [Indispensable.]

E. HERTSLET. *The Map of Africa by Treaty.* 3 vols. 3rd ed. 1909. [Indispensable.]

E. HERTSLET. *The Map of Europe by Treaty.* 4 vols. [The standard work in English.]

R. B. MOWAT. *Select Treaties and Documents to illustrate the Development of the Modern European States-System.* Oxford University Press. 1915. [This valuable little book, at the price of 1s. 6d., is indispensable to the student.]

ECONOMIC GEOGRAPHY

G. G. CHISHOLM. *Handbook of Commercial Geography.* 7th ed.

J. G. BARTHOLOMEW. *Atlas of the World's Commerce.* [A large and exhaustive atlas.]

J. G. BARTHOLOMEW. *Economic Atlas.* With Introduction by L. W. Lyde. Oxford ; The Clarendon Press. [A smaller edition of the above.]

GENERAL WORKS

Stanford's Compendium of Geography and Travel. (By various experts.) [The volumes on Europe, Africa and Asia, by G. G. Chisholm and A. H. Keane respectively.]

LAVISSE ET RAMBAUD. *Histoire générale.* Vols. viii–xii. (In French.)

The Cambridge Modern History. Vols. viii–xii. [The bibliographies in these two works furnish a complete reference to the historical literature from 1789 to the present day.]

A. TOYNBEE. *Nationality and the War.* [A suggestive analysis, particularly of the racial and political problems, with helpful maps.]

The War and Democracy. By R. W. Seton-Watson and other writers. [A very suggestive volume of essays, with full and practical directions on the most useful works of reference.]

The following are the most useful historical text-books on the period from 1789 to 1900.

E. BOURGEOIS. *Manuel historique de politique étrangère.* Vols. ii and iii. (In French.)

A. DÉBIDOUR. *Histoire diplomatique de l'Europe, 1814–78.* 2 vols. (In French.)

W. ALISON PHILLIPS. *Modern Europe, 1815–99.*

C. M. ANDREWS. *The Historical Development of Modern Europe.*

C. D. HAZEN. *Europe since 1815.*

J. H. ROSE. *The Revolutionary and Napoleonic Era.*

J. H. ROSE. *The Development of the European Nations, 1870–1900.*

H. MORSE STEPHENS. *Revolutionary Europe, 1789–1815.*

C. SEIGNOBOS. *Political History of Contemporary Europe since 1814.* (2 vols. Eng. Transl.)

C. A. FYFFE. *Modern Europe from 1792–1878.*

The best purely modern atlas for reference work is Stieler's *Hand-Atlas* (10th ed.). The English edition bears the title of *Stieler's Atlas of Modern Geography.*

HISTORICAL ATLAS

Plates 1-IV serve as a general introduction to the Plates of special areas that follow. They are intended to emphasize and illustrate factors and elements which are an essential part of historical and political geography. It is obvious that no student of politics can neglect in the examination of any single problem in isolation, or of any single problem in relation to other problems, the influence of physical features as revealed in an orographical map, or the racial and economic factors; while the distribution and comparative density of population are complementary to any study of the economic factor. Neglect, indeed, of these elements in historical and political geography has been largely responsible for the failures of many European political settlements. Conspicuous examples are the elaborate arrangements embodied in the work of the Congresses at Vienna (1814-15) and, to a less degree only because the area affected was smaller, in the Treaties of the Congress at Berlin in 1878. But every one of the Plates that follow provides illuminating illustrations, e.g. the partitions and settlement of Poland (Plates XXVII and XXVIII) and the Belgian and Dutch questions (Plate X).

Plate 1 broadly puts a difficult question. The characteristics of the physiographical configuration of Europe as a whole can be classified and grasped by geographical analysis; but how far and in what sense can we say that there are such realities as 'natural' or 'scientific' frontiers, or that the political frontiers of the States of Europe have conformed to the physical features, or are likely to do so with success, i.e. providing thereby a guarantee of stability and permanence? The evidence of facts, as revealed even in the hundred and fifty years covered by this atlas, is both contradictory and bewildering. The Pyrenees are the only mountain range that seems to have provided a permanent frontier in modern history. Neither the Alps, the Carpathians, nor the Balkans have done so. And the same conclusion is suggested by the great rivers, such as the Rhine, the Danube, and the Vistula. The Rhine was not a frontier in 1789, nor is it to-day; the Danube has only been a frontier in parts of its course both in the past and in 1914: the Poland of the eighteenth century and the Poland of to-day have never made the Vistula a frontier. It seems easier to build up a state round a great river than to make that river a boundary. No ethnographical map on a comparatively small scale can do full justice to the intricacy of the racial problem; even on a large scale it cannot represent with scientific precision the interpenetration of racial groups by each other, a result which every economic advance and improvement in the means of communication necessarily tend to increase. And in all ethnographical maps one feature is conspicuously absent, because it is practically impossible to give it satisfactory cartographical representation, viz. the Jews. For every state and area has Jews, the percentage and social and civic status of whom vary enormously according to the area and state under consideration. But apart from these important and misleading drawbacks—common to all ethnographical maps—Plate III suggests and supports one important conclusion, apart from the variety of races that it reveals. In western and central Europe the racial blocks are large, comparatively well defined, and comparatively homogeneous; but in eastern and south-eastern Europe in particular, we have groups rather than blocks, and groups frequently neither large, well defined, nor homogeneous. The best illustration of this will be found by study of Plate XVIII, combined with an attempt to draw political frontiers in confor-

mity with the racial and physiographical features. The problem reaches its maximum of difficulty in Macedonia and Albania. In short, what seems inevitable in western and central Europe seems impossible in south-eastern Europe—the nationalist state based on homogeneity of race and civilization. Plates II and IV provide the material for considering how far modern economic and industrial evolution have revolutionized the political problems of the old Europe of the *ancien régime*. That evolution, in Europe as in Great Britain, has been largely conditioned by the presence or absence of the staple mineral resources of modern industry, e.g. coal, iron, copper, &c., and the degree of utilization of these by organized communities. The congestion of population at certain centres or over certain areas could, in fact, be predicted from a geological map without the aid of a supplementary map showing distribution and density of population. The broad result is that in 1914 the student is dealing with a Europe fundamentally different from that of 1789. Industrialization has radically altered the whole scale of political 'values', and three aspects, out of many, of this alteration may be emphasized here: (1) The political worth and importance of many areas have been conspicuously changed. As examples may be cited the Rhenish provinces acquired by Prussia in 1815, the north-eastern departments of France, modern Belgium, and the province of Silesia. All these previously to 1789 had a definable political importance, particularly as interpreted in terms of military strategy or geographical extent; but their transference to-day to other hands would involve consequences that would fundamentally alter the economic strength of the states from or to which they were transferred, and for very different reasons to those recognized between 1770 and 1815. (2) Industrialization has increased economic interdependence, and made intercommunication an essential of all state and social life. The international control of the great routes of communication provided by rivers practically began with the Congress of Vienna in 1814-15. Every decade since 1815 has added to the tentative steps taken then, and the extension of that international control in the interests of all states and peoples is one of the most urgent items in the political programme of the future. (3) Closely connected with this is the heightened importance of access to the sea, and, through the inland seas, of unimpeded access to the oceans. The higher the degree of industrialization, the more imperative the demand for and need of that unimpeded access. Hence, for states whose industrialization has only just begun or is comparatively undeveloped, access to the sea has come to be regarded as an essential preliminary to advance. For access to the sea means economic independence as well as access to potential markets by the cheapest route and the importation of the raw material of different climatic conditions necessary to a higher industrialization. The demand and the need take many forms: e.g. Can the present political position of the Scheldt be maintained? What is the future of the Kiel Canal? Ought the Dardanelles and the Bosphorus not to be 'liberated'? Can there be a stable and powerful Austria if Trieste and Fiume pass out of Austrian hands? If the Suez Canal is internationalized, what is to be the position of the western access to the Mediterranean? and so forth. These and many other similar questions are political problems which derive their reality from economic needs and conditions,

Plates V and VI deal with the political distribution of power in the Mediterranean. In length about 2,200 miles, in breadth at its greatest 500–600 miles, and covering an area of 900,000 square miles, the Mediterranean is the largest inland sea in the world, with access to three other inland seas (Marmora, Black Sea, and Azov). There is but one natural access to and outlet from the Mediterranean, viz. by the Straits of Gibraltar; the other access by water, the Suez Canal, an achievement of modern science, is not yet fifty years old. The Mediterranean forms a separate and definable area by itself, whether regarded from the point of view of geography or history, and the remarkable combination of characteristics which it unites has conferred on it from the dawn of history to the present day an importance which it is impossible to exaggerate or to exhaust by analysis and illustration. The history of the Mediterranean from the days of Phoenicia, Crete, and Greece to our own time is a history of western civilized mankind. Mastery of the Mediterranean means mastery of an area in which the climate, natural resources, and routes of communication both from north to south and from east to west confer the secrets and the keys of political, naval, and economic power.

The waters of the Mediterranean wash the shores of three continents—Europe, Asia, and Africa—but the physical configuration of this vast area cuts it off from these continents and constitutes it a single region by itself. Broadly, that area is divided into two basins, a western and an eastern, the dividing-point being the island of Sicily. Access from one basin to the other is provided (a) by the narrow Straits of Messina, (b) by the Straits of Tunis or of Sicily, about a hundred miles wide, with the island of Malta lying across the route. The western basin is girdled by a practically continuous wall of mountains, pierced by the Straits of Gibraltar and the accesses to the hinterlands behind the walls provided by the valley of the Ebro, the Gate of Carcassonne, the valley of the Rhône, and the passes and routes to central Europe north of the city of Genoa. Of the accesses by land, the Gate of Carcassonne and the valley of the Rhône are the most important. The eastern basin is not so continuously girdled by mountains, and the shores are cut into deep and big gulfs. The peculiar configuration of the peninsula of Gallipoli, with the Dardanelles and the Straits of the Bosphorus giving access to the Black Sea and south-eastern Europe, invests the Aegean and Constantinople with a special importance. Quite recently the construction of the Suez Canal has fundamentally altered the south-eastern littoral, since it has linked the Mediterranean with the Red Sea and all the direct water routes to the East.

With the alteration in shipbuilding that dates from the end of the sixteenth century and marks the rise of English and Dutch sea-power, countries that are non-Mediterranean in geographical position have been able to compete with the strictly Mediterranean states and exercise a decisive influence in the struggle for, and the distribution of, political and economic power. The entry of England into the Mediterranean is perhaps the capital fact of the seventeenth century, and the establishment of British power at Gibraltar and Minorca by the Treaties of Utrecht (1713) coincides with the waning of Ottoman sea-power, which had reached its height in the sixteenth century. No less significant was the withdrawal of Great Britain in 1756 with the dramatic re-entry in 1798 and the 'Battle of the Nile'.

A study of the map in 1789 reveals at once that neither in the western nor the eastern basin had any single Power established a complete control. Great Britain had definitively lost Minorca (1783), but retained Gibraltar. The Bourbon states of Spain, France, and Naples (the Two Sicilies) dominate the northern arc of the littoral of the western basin; but Genoa is still an independent republic; Tuscany is a Habsburg possession; Malta is in the possession of the Knights of St. John; the African coast is in the hands of the Moroccans of the Rif, and the Barbary states of Algiers, Tunis, and Tripoli, nominally vassal states of the Ottoman empire, practically independent piratical communities whose ferocious depredations on commerce, and particularly Christian commerce, made them a scourge and an intolerable scandal. In the eastern basin Venice, with her Dalmatian provinces, controlled the Adriatic, while the remainder of the littoral belonged to Turkish power, at sea but a shadow of what it had been. The steady advance of British power in India made Egypt (a vassal province of the Turkish empire) an area of exceptional concern for British policy. The age of Napoleon revived the great effort of Bourbon France to make the Mediterranean a French lake, and the struggle focussed itself on the vital points and areas—Sicily, Malta, the Ionian Isles, Constantinople, and Egypt. Napoleon's failure to secure these decided the issue in the Mediterranean, and subsequently on the Continent behind the walls of the Mediterranean. The settlement in 1815 of Europe as a whole—an equilibrium and balance of power—is mirrored and repeated in the Mediterranean map, Gibraltar, Malta, and the Protectorate of the Ionian Isles represent the share of the premier sea-power; France retains Corsica and her two great accesses through the Gate of Carcassonne and the valley of the Rhône; the Ottoman empire still sprawls round the eastern basin: Sicily has been reunited with the restored Bourbon kingdom of Naples; the kingdom of Sardinia (Piedmont) has absorbed Genoa; but Habsburg power has definitely established itself also by absorbing Venetia and the Dalmatian littoral. The Barbary states remained as they were in 1789. Since 1815 the whole situation has been profoundly altered: (1) The Barbary states have disappeared; Algiers and Algeria, Tunis and Tunisia have fallen to France; the Morocco of the Rif has become Spanish; the unification of Italy has placed the whole Italian peninsula under a single control; Sicily and Sardinia are Italian, and Tripoli has also passed into Italian hands. (2) If Austria has lost Lombardy and Venetia she has strengthened her grip on the four important Adriatic harbours of Trieste, Fiume, Pola, and Cattaro. (3) The Ionian Isles and Crete have passed to the new kingdom of Greece, which also (1913) has secured Salonica, commanding the one great land route from the Aegean to central Europe. (4) The Ottoman empire retains the Dardanelles and the Bosphorus and thereby blocks the free access of Russia to the Mediterranean. (5) Cyprus (1878) has been placed under British occupation, and in 1914, however difficult it may be to define it in international law, Egypt is practically a British Protectorate. These main changes only embody results and movements, the causes and evolution of which must be sought elsewhere. Of the main problems presented by the map in 1914, three may be noted here: (1) How long will the Turk maintain his existence in Europe and retain the unique Mediterranean position in the eastern basin that Constantinople, the Dardanelles, and the Bosphorus confer? If he is displaced, who will take his place? (2) The construction of 'the Bagdad railway' terminating on the Persian Gulf is a deliberate scheme to give south-eastern Europe (under German control) a direct route to the East, independent of Mediterranean conditions. But before such a railway can be made, the question of Constantinople and the Persian Gulf must be definitely settled. Constantinople at one end and Basra at the other are in 1914 Turkish: how long will they remain so? (3) The united German empire, consummated in 1871, has no direct and unimpeded access to or position on the Mediterranean. And this is also true of the Russian empire. The map, in short, shows that two of the great European states are at present excluded from the greatest inland sea in the world. The economic, no less than the political and naval, significance of this exclusion may be explained or estimated differently by different students. But its bearing on all the problems of modern European life, to which the Mediterranean is as important to-day as it has ever been in the past, cannot be neglected. And whatever the answer may be, it will contribute to decide other problems than the one raised by the exclusion itself.

Plates VII, VIII, IX should be studied together, and here, as in the other Plates, it is only possible to comment on the most significant features of the political evolution. Details must be worked out in the standard authorities. Plate VII exhibits the France of the Bourbon monarchy, of the *ancien régime* on the eve of the fundamental reconstruction wrought by the Revolutionary epoch. Politically, it is a fairly homogeneous block. Alsace had been acquired in 1648, Strasburg in 1681 (confirmed in 1684), and the frontier to the north-east broadly represents that settled in 1713. Since then Lorraine, the reversion of which had been assigned to France in 1736, had been absorbed in 1766, and Corsica had been acquired in 1768—one year before the birth of Napoleon, who was thus born a French subject. Within the frontier line the territory of Avignon and the Venaissin was under the sovereignty of the Pope. French effort, in the eighteenth century, to complete the work of Louis XIV and advance to ' the natural ' frontier of the Rhine eastwards, had failed, and the boundary line between France and the Austrian Netherlands (the modern Belgium) was an arbitrary political line, drawn by a group of treaties. But if the France of 1789 was a political homogeneity, the governmental, administrative, judicial, and fiscal divisions were extraordinarily complicated, confused, and conflicting. The administrative areas did not correspond with the judicial, nor the judicial with the fiscal, and across all three lay the ecclesiastical divisions. Moreover, both in Lorraine and in Alsace there existed a network of imperial feudal rights and jurisdictions, connected with the organization of ' Germany ' under the Emperor of the Holy Roman empire of the German nation. A series of maps would be required (such as those in Schrader's atlas) to illustrate the diversity, lack of unification and symmetry, that underlie the deceptive uniformity of the political map. It must suffice here to note (1) the three fiscal divisions : (a) the *cinq grosses fermes* subject to the tariff of 1664 ; (b) the *provinces réputées étrangères* outside that tariff ; and (c) the *étranger effectif* acquired since 1664 or specially privileged. (2) The division into thirty-eight governments under governors. (3) The division into thirty intendances or *généralités* under an intendant. (4) The judicial areas, the centre of which were the thirteen parliaments or chief judicial courts.

The Revolutionary and Napoleonic epoch swept all these obstacles to a real unification away, and embarked Revolutionary France on a series of wars of conquest, the results of which reached their climax in 1810. Plate VIII represents the ' grand Empire français ' under Napoleon at its height, when Napoleon could truly claim to be master of western and central Europe. The France of 1810 has advanced a long way beyond the ' natural frontiers ' of Alps, Pyrenees, and the Rhine. It has annexed the modern Belgium and Holland, north-western Germany between the Ems and the Elbe, nearly one-half of northern Italy, Tuscany, and the major part of the Papal States, the south-eastern and Dalmatian (Illyrian) provinces of ' Austria ', and the city of Danzig, at the mouth of the Vistula. In addition, imperial France controlled through the Confederation of the Rhine the whole of central Germany, through the kingdom of Italy the remainder of the northern and central parts of the Italian peninsula, and through the grand duchy of Warsaw (a Napoleonic creation) the kingdom of Prussia and the empire of Austria. Europe, in fact, as a system of independent and sovereign states had in 1810 ceased to exist. Plate IX represents the position of France in 1814 and in 1815, after the fall of Napoleon and the collapse of the Napoleonic empire. Its frontiers are practically those of 1789 before the wars of the Revolution. The Bourbon king was restored to the France over which his predecessors had ruled. Some trifling alterations were made (and slightly revised after Napoleon's return and second downfall), viz. : the addition of Venaissin and Avignon, a strip of Belgian territory, a strip of German territory at Landau and Saarbrück, the north-western portion of Savoy (Chambéry and Annecy) as defined in the final Treaty of November 20, 1815. On the other hand, the Prussian demand for the restoration of Alsace and Lorraine to German sovereignty was refused by the allied governments.

Since that date France in Europe has made two moderate acquisitions and suffered one significant loss. In 1860 Napoleon acquired, in compensation for his aid to Italy in the wars of 1859 and his acquiescence in the political changes that resulted from it, the province of Nice (Alpes-Maritimes) and Italian Savoy. In 1871, by the Treaty of Frankfort (May 10), as the result of the Franco-German War, France ceded to the new German empire Alsace (with the exception of the fortress of Belfort, commanding the easiest route, 'The Gap of Belfort', from south-western Germany across the Rhine) and the larger part of Lorraine, including the great fortress of Metz.

It is no less significant that between 1815 and 1870 various efforts of successive French governments to extend their eastward frontier failed. In 1830 the modern kingdom of Belgium retained the boundaries laid down in 1815 ; and the ambition of Napoleon III, to acquire either Luxemburg or any portion of the Rhenish lands between the Meuse, the Rhine, and the French frontier was frustrated. The loss, however, of Alsace and Lorraine is, in its political significance and consequences, the outstanding feature of Plate IX. But no summary of the French position in 1914 would be adequate which did not emphasize the remarkable growth of France and French power outside Europe, which began in 1830 with the gradual acquisition of Algeria, and which in 1914 has left her the second colonial power in the world. (See particularly Plates VI, XXXIV, XXXV, and XXXVI.)

Plate X. The modern kingdom of Holland, as a monarchical state, dates from 1814 ; the kingdom of Belgium, both in its area, character, and international status, is a purely modern creation of the nineteenth century. Broadly speaking, the territorial area of the Holland and Belgium of 1830 was in the sixteenth century represented by the seventeen provinces of the Netherlands which had passed under the rule of the Emperor Charles V of the House of Habsburg as heir of the House of Burgundy. Philip II, King of Spain, as Charles's successor, inherited the Netherlands, while the imperial crown passed to the Austrian branch of the Habsburg line. The revolt of the Netherlands resulted (1584) in the formation of the northern portion into the independent Republic of the United Netherlands under the Stadtholdership of the House of Orange. The southern or Belgic portion—the Low Countries—remained under the sovereignty of the Crown of Spain (the Spanish Habsburgs) until 1714, when the Spanish Netherlands were transferred to the Austrian branch of the Habsburgs and became the Austrian Netherlands. Thus in 1789 we have: (1) The Dutch Republic of the United Netherlands (viz. the original eight revolting provinces of 1584—Holland, Zeeland, Utrecht, Guelderland, Zutphen, Overyssel, Friesland, Gröningen, with the lands of the Generality (State-Flanders and State-Brabant) and State-Limburg, and State-Upper-Guelderland) ; (2) the Austrian Netherlands proper ; (3) the duchy of Luxemburg (included in the Austrian Netherlands) ; (4) the prince-bishopric of Liège, an ecclesiastical principality of the Holy Roman empire. The acquisition of (2), (3), (4) from the reign of Louis XIV onwards (1643) was a permanent object of French policy, as it would advance the French frontier to the Rhine and give the French monarchy the control of the Scheldt and a big piece of coast-line on the Channel and the North Sea, and was consistently opposed by Great Britain. The French Revolution and Napoleon accomplished what Louis XIV and Louis XV had failed to secure. Conquered by French arms, the Austrian Netherlands and Liège were incorporated with France in 1797, and the remodelled Batavian Republic took the place of the United Netherlands. In 1807 Napoleon transformed the Republic into the kingdom of Holland for his brother Louis, and in 1811 annexed it to France.

In 1815 a fresh settlement was made in order to establish a strong barrier against French advance on the vulnerable north-eastern frontier. A single kingdom of the United Netherlands was constituted under the restored rule of the House of Orange-Nassau : this included the old Austrian Netherlands, Liège, the duchy of Luxemburg, and the former Dutch Republic. The revolt of the southern portion in 1830 resulted in 1839, after complicated and lengthy negotiations, in a wholly new arrangement : (1) Two kingdoms were set up—(a) Holland, representing the historic Dutch state, (b) Belgium, a new creation under Leopold I of the Saxe-Coburg House ; (2) western Luxemburg was annexed to Belgium, eastern, retaining the title of the duchy, was assigned to the Dutch king ; (c) Limburg, with the important fortress of Maestricht, was enlarged and assigned to Holland ; along with Luxemburg, it was included in the German Confederation as organized in 1815 ; (d) Belgium was made perpetually neutral and its neutrality guaranteed by the international Treaty of April 19, 1839, to which Great Britain, France, Austria, Prussia, and Russia were parties.

Three changes since that date must be noted. In 1867 a proposal to cede the duchy of Luxemburg, as defined in 1839, to France by purchase met with strong opposition in Germany and was not carried through. In its place (1) Luxemburg was severed from all political connexion with the new North German Confederation, its fortifications were razed, and it was neutralized under the collective guarantee of the Great Powers, while the duchy itself remained under the rule of the House of Orange-Nassau, reigning in Holland (May 11, 1867); (2) at the same time Dutch Limburg was also severed from its former political connexion with Germany and made an integral part of Holland ; (3) in 1890, on the death of the King of Holland, Luxemburg, by the operation of the Salic Law, passed from the Crown of Holland, inherited by the present Queen Wilhelmina, to the nearest male heir of the House of Orange-Nassau. It therefore became an independent grand duchy, whose perpetual neutrality is established by the collective guarantee of the Great Powers.

The modern kingdom of Holland dates only from 1815 or 1807 (if the Napoleonic kingdom is considered), but as an independent state, and as a colonial and commercial power, with a separate history, a great tradition, and a long record of achievement and of independence, asserted and maintained, it dates from the middle of the sixteenth century. The kingdom of Belgium, inheriting the traditions and civilization of separate provinces, each with a separate history, and evolved through many vicissitudes, represents a purely modern fusion, and is both in its name, international status (which it shares with Switzerland and Luxemburg), and area, the creation of the concert of Europe in 1839, working on the material provided by a revolt and shaping its work to meet the ends of European policy—the prevention of this part of Europe, the cockpit of so many bloody struggles for European supremacy, falling into either French or German hands. The nineteenth century, following the example of Napoleon, has been prolific and versatile in kingdom-making. The kingdom of Belgium is younger than the kingdoms of Saxony, Bavaria, and Würtemberg, but older than the kingdoms of Italy, Serbia, Roumania, Bulgaria, Norway, and Montenegro.

As Plates XI, XII, XIII, XIV convincingly reveal, no state or group of states has passed through, from 1789 to 1914, more numerous, continuous, fundamental, and striking changes than Germany. Plate XI confronts the student with a delineation of the Holy Roman empire of the German nation as it existed in 1789, and the broad problem of historical geography is to ascertain how this map has passed into the map of Plate XIII, exhibiting the united German empire of 1914. Only a map or a series of maps on a large scale could do justice to the bewildering tangle of sovereignties, areas, and states, to the interlocking boundaries, conflicting dynasties, and territorial and political antagonisms that Germany in 1789 presents. The leading features alone of this mosaic can be specified here : (1) The empire, as a political organization, consisted of some 360 different parts and members, divided, broadly, into (a) the electorates, whose rulers, the electors, had the right to elect the emperor ; (b) principalities of different kinds ; (c) the free cities ; and (d) the imperial

knights who held their fiefs direct from the emperor. The electorates were nine in number, viz. Bohemia, Brandenburg, the Palatinate, Saxony, Bavaria, Hanover—the lay electorates—and the three ecclesiastical electorates, the archbishoprics of Mainz, Triers (Trèves), and Cologne. The principalities included 4 archbishoprics, 16 bishoprics, 6 abbots, and the two chiefs of the great orders of the Teutonic Knights and the Knights of St. John of Jerusalem at Malta. The Free Cities were 56 in number, of which only 14 had any real importance, viz. Lubeck, Hamburg, Bremen, Goslar, Cologne, Aachen, Worms, Speier, Frankfort, Wetzlar, Regensburg, Nuremberg, Augsburg, and Ulm. Of the territorial powers the most important was the Austrian branch of the House of Habsburg, which had practically established an hereditary right to the imperial crown, and which held under its rule Bohemia, Moravia, Austria proper, Tyrol, the Austrian Netherlands, and scattered possessions in Swabia and Alsace (see also the commentary to Plates XIX–XXI). Second in territorial importance and political power was the kingdom of Prussia, and after it must be placed the great duchy of Bavaria (an electorate), which had united with itself the Palatinate and the duchies of Jülich and Berg, the electorate of Saxony, the electorate of Hanover (united with the Crown of Great Britain), and the duchies of Brunswick, Würtemberg, Baden, Mecklenburg, Oldenburg, the Hesses, and Nassau.

Four further points may be noted : (1) Within the empire (the Reich) were princes who also held territories outside, e. g. East Prussia and the Polish territories of Prussia were not within the empire ; the King of Sweden held Swedish Pomerania ; the King of Denmark outside the empire was Duke of Holstein within it ; and much of the territory of the House of Habsburg was not within the boundaries of the German empire. (2) The Rhine was not a purely German river—it was neither, in the words of a famous song, 'Germany's boundary' nor 'Germany's stream'. Basel in the south was Swiss ; from the mouth to Emmerich was Dutch ; Strasburg and the Alsatian frontier were French. (3) There was no real political capital for the whole of Germany, such as Paris, Madrid, London, Petrograd, are for their respective states—such as Berlin is to-day. It is questionable whether from A.D. 800 until 1871 Germany ever had a capital, the centre of the governmental, political, intellectual, social, and economic life of the whole German people, conscious of its unity. In 1789 neither Berlin, nor Vienna, nor Frankfort, nor Aachen, nor Dresden, nor Munich, fulfilled any of the qualifications that a capital embodies. (4) For two centuries before 1789 three processes are distinctly traceable : a shrinkage of the territory within the German political organization of the empire (e. g. Alsace and Lorraine had been torn away) ; a gradual secularization of the ecclesiastical principalities ; the growth of the larger principalities within the empire at the expense of the smaller, of which 'the Habsburg State' (Austria, as it is conveniently but incorrectly called), Prussia, and Bavaria are the best examples.

On this ramshackle and obsolescent organization the wars of the Revolution and Napoleon administered a series of violent shocks. It is impossible here even to indicate the complicated and shifting changes registered by the Treaties of Campo Formio (1797), Lunéville (1801), Vienna (1805), Tilsit (1807), Schönbrunn (1809), and the Imperial Recess (Reichsdeputationshauptschluss) of 1803. The map of 1810 reveals a new Germany, the main features of which are profoundly significant. The Germany of 1789 has been transformed into four well-marked political areas : (1) The Holy Roman empire has been dissolved (1806) ; the effort to group Germany in a single organization has been abandoned ; the empire of Austria has been created, thrust out of Germany altogether, and established as a separate state (1806). (2) The left bank of the Rhine is now French, and France has also annexed a large area in the north-west between the former Dutch Republic and the Elbe, together with the city of Danzig, commanding the mouth of the Vistula. (3) The kingdom of

Prussia has been deprived (1807) of all its territory west of the Elbe and much of its Polish acquisitions, and is practically only half of what it was in 1805. (4) The rest of Germany has been regrouped and is organized, under French control of its diplomacy and military resources, as the Confederation of the Rhine.

Three other features are also noticeable : (a) the disappearance of many of the small states of 1789 with the growth of the more important secondary states, four of which have become kingdoms, viz. Saxony, Bavaria, Würtemberg, and Westphalia (which included Hanover) ; (b) the secularization of the ecclesiastical states, which have practically disappeared ; (c) the disappearance of the fifty-six imperial free cities. French supremacy in western and central Europe rested, in short, on the lack of unity and the denationalization and dismemberment of Germany, which was further than ever from an effective organization or the possession of a capital as the centre of a German national life.

The settlement of 1815 was only rendered possible by the collapse of the Napoleonic empire and the reduction of France to the boundaries of 1792. No attempt, however, was made to restore the Holy Roman empire or to bring the whole of Germany under a single and effective political control, as demanded by the pioneers of national unification. The Confederation of 1815, consisting of thirty-nine sovereign states, resembles rather the Confederation of the Rhine with the reconstituted empire of Austria and the reconstituted kingdom of Prussia included, while the territorial partition between these thirty-nine members was assisted by the recovery of lands that had been lost to Germany since 1792. Within this Federation of States—not in any true sense a Federal State—there were three Germanies : the empire of Austria, the kingdom of Prussia, and the states that are neither Austrian nor Prussian, which made a middle Germany, the most important members of which were the kingdoms of Bavaria, Saxony, Würtemberg, and Hanover (created a kingdom in 1815 and until 1837 united with the British Crown). As in 1789, non-German powers were represented in the Confederation, e. g. the King of Holland holding Luxemburg and Limburg, the King of Denmark holding Holstein. And, as in 1789, both Prussia and Austria contained territories not included in the Confederation. Four of the old free cities—Hamburg, Lübeck, Bremen, and Frankfort—were restored and made members of the Confederation, the presidency of which was assigned to Austria. It is out of this loosely-jointed Confederation that the modern German empire has been evolved. No important changes in the map took place until the second Danish war of 1864 started a series of developments which were completed in seven dramatic years. This was essentially the work of Prussia. The second Danish war wrested both Schleswig and Holstein from Danish sovereignty (October 1864) ; in 1866 came the Prussian declaration of the dissolution of the Confederation and the war with Austria for supremacy in Germany. The Peace of Prague (August 1866) thrust Austria (as in 1806) out of Germany altogether, and left Prussia, increased by important annexations (see below) to form a new North German Confederation, under Prussian presidency. This (June 19, 1867) was composed of twenty-two members—the line of the river Main being taken broadly as the southern frontier, while the three southern states of Bavaria, Würtemberg, and Baden were left to form a Southern Confederation, which they did not do, though all three entered into a separate military and economic union with the North German Confederation. The defeat of France in the war of 1870 and the Treaty of Frankfort (May 10, 1871) put the coping-stone to the federal unification of 1867, which had been preceded (January 18, 1871) by the scene in the Galerie des Glaces of Louis XIV at Versailles, when the King of Prussia was proclaimed German Emperor of a united Germany. Bavaria, Würtemberg, Baden, and the part of Hesse outside the North German Confederation, were admitted to the new German empire created by adding the southern states to the organization of 1867. The new imperial crown was vested as an hereditary right

in the monarchy of Prussia, as President of the Confederation. The Prussian King, it should be noted, is Emperor in Germany, or German Emperor, not Emperor of Germany. Alsace and Lorraine, ceded by France, were not annexed to Prussia, nor added as a separate state to the organization. They were treated as imperial territory (Reichsland), governed by a vicegerent responsible to the imperial government and only sharing to a limited extent in the Federal Constitution. Since 1871 no addition, save Heligoland, ceded by Great Britain in 1891, has been made to the territories of the German empire in Europe.

Plate XIV summarizes the main phases of the evolution and expansion of the kingdom of Prussia, which is the most remarkable feature of modern German history. In 1789 that kingdom consisted of three well-marked areas, separated from each other by non-Prussian territory : (a) the Rhenish provinces ; (b) the central nucleus which had grown up round the original core of Prussia, viz. the old mark and electorate of Brandenburg, with Berlin as its capital ; and (c) the duchy of East Prussia, successfully wrested from Polish suzerainty in 1660. To these Frederick the Great had added East Friesland, Silesia, and West Prussia (excepting Danzig), thereby linking up the central and eastern areas. Further extensive additions of purely Polish territory were made by Prussia's share in the partitions of 1793 and 1795 (see Plate XXVII) and by smaller Prussian annexations to the west between 1803 and 1806.

In 1807, however, the disastrous campaign of Jena and the Treaty of Tilsit reduced Prussia to its political nadir. She lost all her territory west of the Elbe, as well as her Polish acquisitions of 1793 and 1795, including Danzig, and retained only the lands between the Elbe and Oder, Pomerania, Silesia, and East Prussia. Eight years of humiliation and dismemberment followed, and then the reconstitution of Germany in 1815 brought a new Prussia into existence. In the east she recovered Thorn and her share of Poland, acquired in 1793 (the modern province of Posen) ; in the centre, Swedish Pomerania, the Altmark, half of the kingdom of Saxony, and portions of Thuringia, and in the west a large addition to her former Rhenish provinces. She was now not only the chief state in northern Germany, but the most important purely Germanic state in the new Confederation of 1815. After half a century of patient internal reorganization and development Prussia made a bid for supremacy. On the defeat of Austria in the war of 1866 she annexed Schleswig and Holstein and Lauenburg (ceded by Denmark), together with Hanover, East Friesland, the electorate of Hesse, Nassau, part of the Grand Duchy of Hesse, and the city of Frankfort, thereby becoming far the largest of the German states and the head of the new North German Confederation created by herself out of the organization of 1815. Since 1867 (save for Heligoland) no additions have been made to the Prussian kingdom, which has been built up since the accession of Frederick the Great (1740) mainly out of the annexations from other German states. The supremacy of Prussia in the modern German empire does not rest merely on the position and powers assigned to the monarchy in the constitution. Prussia has given Germany a capital, Berlin, the largest town in the empire, the centre of imperial and Prussian government, the seat of the most important German university, and of the Imperial Parliament (Reichstag), the head-quarters of the Prussian army, the Imperial Navy, and the Imperial Bank. The census of 1910 shows that Prussia has 134,000 out of 298,000 square miles of German territory, 40 millions out of 65 millions of inhabitants, and furnishes 17 out of 26 of the active army corps, 24,000 out of 36,000 miles of railway, and sends 236 out of 397 members to the Reichstag. Prussia, in short, dominates the political, social, intellectual, financial, industrial and military life of the empire.

Plate XV. The Swiss Confederation of 1789 was composed of three elements : (1) The Thirteen Cantons, which had come into existence between 1291 and 1513 as a league of defence against a common foe—the Habsburgs. Practically independent by 1513, their formal separation from, and independence of, the Holy Roman empire was recognized in 1648. (2) *Allied Districts*, i. e. areas in varying degrees of alliance with the thirteen cantons, but not enjoying the full political membership of the Confederation. (3) *Subject Districts*, i. e. areas ruled by the cantons which had brought them into political subjection. After 1789 the first important change was in 1803, when Napoleon, by the Act of Mediation, gave the title of Switzerland to a new organization on a republican basis. This was composed of nineteen cantons (the thirteen original cantons, whose territories were rearranged, and six new cantons, viz. Grisons, St. Gall, Aargau, Thurgau, Ticino, and Vaud), to whose territory was also added (1802) the Frickthal, ceded by Austria. Two of the new cantons came from the former 'allied', four from the former 'subject' districts; and it is notable that they brought into the Confederation, which until 1789 was composed wholly of German-speaking members, both Italian-speaking and French-speaking districts on terms of political equality. The Congress of Vienna in 1815 completed the constitution and organization of modern Switzerland : it added three new cantons to the nineteen in existence, viz. Valais, Neufchâtel, and Geneva ; and by the Treaty of November 20, 1815, the Great Powers, Austria, France, Great Britain, Prussia, and Russia, which signed the Treaty, ' acknowledged and guaranteed in the most formal manner the neutrality and inviolability of Switzerland, and her independence of all foreign influence', as 'entering into the true interests of the policy of the whole of Europe'. Of the new cantons, Neufchâtel was in a peculiar position, for though it was a full member of the Swiss Republic, it remained under the sovereignty of the King of Prussia until 1857, when the king renounced his claim. Since 1815, with the exception of some trifling frontier rectifications, there have been no changes in the territorial boundaries of Switzerland. In 1833 the cantons of Basel was divided into two parts—Basel city and the rural districts, Baselland. In 1846 the seven Roman Catholic cantons formed a separate League—the Sonderbund—whose secession from the main body was only frustrated by a short and sharp civil war, in which the Sonderbund was decisively defeated. The subsequent changes and reform of the constitution on strictly federal lines belong, however, to Swiss and European history and have not affected the political features of the map.

Plates XVI, XVII exhibit the phases through which the Italian peninsula from 1789 onwards has, in a century, achieved political unification, and entered for the first time in modern history the European state system as a single and united kingdom. Italy in 1789, no less than in 1815, was ' a geographical expression ', and the area of the peninsula was divided between a number of principalities, the result of centuries of complicated development and European invasion. In the north there is (a) the kingdom of Sardinia or Piedmont, representing the growth of the territories of the House of Savoy since 1418 ; (b) the duchy of Milan, an imperial fief, which had passed from Spain to the House of Austria ; (c) the republics of Genoa, Lucca, San Marino, and Venice, the latter of which still retained her Dalmatian territories on the eastern littoral of the Adriatic ; (d) the duchies of Mantua, Parma (Austrian), and of Modena, under rulers dynastically connected with the House of Habsburg ; (e) the duchy of Tuscany, transferred to the House of Lorraine when Lorraine was ceded to France, and now an appanage for the younger members of the Austrian Habsburgs ; (f) the Papal territories, which included Bologna, Romagna, and the Legations ; and (g) the kingdom of the Two Sicilies, i.e. Naples and Sicily, transferred in 1735 to a branch of the Bourbon dynasty. Italy thus represented the balance of power in Europe, and was a singular medley of monarchical, princely, ecclesiastical, and republican rule. The revolutionary and Napoleonic epoch introduced changes as startling and dramatic as those in Germany which broke down the barriers and divisions of the eighteenth century and foreshadowed the

possibility of a real unification. By 1810 Italy had become virtually a French province. Savoy and Piedmont, Genoa, Parma, Tuscany, the Papal territories round Rome, were incorporated into France ; the Papacy had ceased to rule at Rome ; the republics of Genoa and Venice had been suppressed ; the kingdom of Naples on the mainland had been wrested from the Bourbons and given first to Napoleon's brother Joseph and then to Marshal Murat, married to Napoleon's sister, Caroline. The islands of Sardinia and Sicily alone remained under their former rulers. Most significant perhaps of all, a kingdom of Italy formed out of Milan, Modena, Mantua, the Papal Legations, and Venetian territories, had been set up under the rule of Eugène de Beauharnais, Napoleon's step-son. It is notable that the frontier of this kingdom on the north included the Italian-speaking part of Tyrol (hitherto Austrian), and reached the Isonzo to the east—two facts which the Italy of to-day has not forgotten.

The reconstitution of Europe in 1815 registered a deliberate effort to restore Italy to the conditions and political demarcation of 1789, as a comparison of Plates XVI and XVII very clearly brings out. The kingdom of Naples, the Papal state and the duchy of Tuscany were restored to their former rulers, practically without modification. Of the former republics the tiny San Marino alone remained, and remains so to-day. Genoa was incorporated in an enlarged kingdom of Piedmont. Parma, Lucca, and Modena were retained as separate principalities. Austria took as her share Lombardy and Venetia, the portions of Tyrol in the Napoleonic kingdom of Italy being restored to the Tyrolese area. Italy was once again a mosaic of states, from 1815 onwards controlled by the predominance of Austria, whose power rested on her grip on the north and her determination to govern by dividing and denationalizing the forces that made for unity.

This settlement (with the exception of a small change in 1847, when Lucca was incorporated in Tuscany and the Duke of Lucca became Duke of Parma) lasted until 1859, when the kingdom of Piedmont, in alliance with the France of Napoleon III, came forward as the champion of an ' Italy for the Italians '. The Treaty of Villafranca (1860) gave Lombardy west of the Mincio to Piedmont (Austria retaining eastern Lombardy and Venetia), while Piedmont ceded to France Nice and Savoy. In 1860 the greater portion of central Italy had voluntarily joined the new Piedmont, the ruling houses fled or were expelled, and the Papacy as a temporal power was reduced to the Patrimony of St. Peter. In the same year Garibaldi's famous expedition freed Naples and Sicily from Bourbon rule, and on March 17, 1861, King Victor Emmanuel at Turin revived the title of King of Italy. There remained only the Austrian territories in the north, and Rome and the Papal territory in the centre, outside the new kingdom. The war of 1866, with Prussia as an ally against Austria, brought the cession of eastern Lombardy and Venetia, and finally, on September 20, 1870, the Italian troops entered the Holy City ; the Papacy ceased to exist as a temporal power, and Rome became the capital of a united Italy. A new national, monarchical state had in eleven years been added to the European system.

Italy's share in European politics and her expansion across the Mediterranean have not so far altered the frontiers established in 1859 and in 1866. But, as Plate XVII indicates, the recovery of 'unredeemed Italy' (*Italia irredenta*) is, and remains, an object of Italian ambition and national ideals. A restoration of the frontier lines of the Italian kingdom of 1810 to the north would practically incorporate the Italian-speaking part of Tyrol, but a study of Plates III and XVIII shows that a frontier line to the east drawn on ethnological divisions, opens up formidable political and economic difficulties, in which Italian claims either of race, sentiment, military strategy, or historic tradition are only one element and are in conflict with the claims of other historic groups and organizations no less insistent and deserving of the weightiest consideration.

Plates XVIII-XXV have for their subject-matter the labyrinth of problems concentrated in south-eastern Europe. The region represented by a line drawn from the Moravian Gate through Passau to Trieste, bounded by the Carpathians in the north and the river Pruth and Constantinople to the east and southwards to Crete and the Aegean Islands, is a palimpsest on which successive empires and races have written in successive layers their indelible and conflicting records. South-eastern Europe, indeed, is an area in which the ghosts of the past are as active as the living minds of the present, and in which the dust of the dead centuries is perennially flowering into the ideals of the future. Modern Hellenism, for example, given substance by the creation of the kingdom of Greece in 1830, has its roots deep in 'the glory that was Greece' in the days of Periclean Athens, or the splendour that was Byzantium in the days of the Iconoclast emperors. And across the welter of racial conflict, expressed in Plate XVIII, is spread deep and wide the welter of conflicting religions, which has divided races united by blood and language, as is perhaps best seen in the separation of the Roman Catholic Croat from the Orthodox Serb. The history of south-eastern Europe proves that loyalty to a church and a faith may be a more potent unifier even than an inherited race-memory or a common speech. On the struggle between allegiance to Rome or to Byzantium—between the Latin Church of the west and the Greek Church of the east, dating from the third century A.D.—was superimposed in 1453 by the capture of Constantinople, the struggle between the Crescent and the Cross.

The evolution of the modern empire of Austria is an essential part of 'the (Near) Eastern Question'. Metternich, in his autobiography, has pointed out first that 'Austria is like no other kingdom in its origin or its maturity', secondly that until 1806, when the rulers took the title of 'Emperor of Austria', the correct name for what we conveniently call Austria (really only the title of the archduchy) was 'The House of Austria' or 'The House of Habsburg in Austria'—' a case unique in the history of states, for in no other country has the name of the ruling family been used, instead of the name of the country in ordinary, still less in diplomatic, usage.' 'Austria', then, is only an incorrect term (until 1806) for a group of territories differing in race, language, institutions, traditions, religion, and their past, which in a process extending over six centuries were by 1789 united by having a common ruler. The political importance and significance of this unique state in 1789 governed by the head of the House of Habsburg in Austria were derived mainly from four different elements: (1) The imperial title, as Emperor in the Holy Roman empire, which had been practically hereditary (in theory still elective) since the fifteenth century in the male heir of the Austrian Habsburgs. As emperor he was the head of the imperial organization of Germany. (2) The numerous possessions in different parts of Europe, over which he ruled, not as emperor, but as the ruler of territory whose sovereignty had been acquired by marriage, inheritance, or conquest. A full list of these titles would fill a page of small print. It must suffice to note that the Head of the Habsburgs in 1789 was sovereign in the Austrian Netherlands (Belgium), Duke of Luxemburg, Seigneur of German territories (Falkenstein and in the Breisgau), Duke of Milan, Mantua and Tuscany in Italy, Prince-Count of Voralberg and Tirol, Duke of Styria, Carinthia, and Carniola, Archduke of Austria (proper), Margrave of Moravia, Apostolic King of Hungary, King of Bohemia, Croatia, Slavonia, Galicia, and Lodomeria, Grand Prince of Transylvania, and Duke of Bukowina. These possessions gave the Habsburg House political interests in every part of Europe. (3) The racial medley (revealed by Plate XVIII) was even more pronounced than it is to-day. In 1789 the Habsburg House ruled over Belgians and Flemings, Germans, Czechs, Slovenes, Slovaks, Magyars, Poles, Ruthenians, Roumanians, Saxons, Italians, Croats—in some parts in well-defined groups, frequently in areas where no single race had a marked predominance. (4) The geographical features of the main block of territories. 'Austria'

was a state built up round the middle Danube from Passau in the west to the Iron Gates at Orsova in the east. To the north the great arc of the Bohemian mountains and the Carpathians sweeping round to Orsova provided a natural frontier and basin; Tyrol and Lombardy down to the line of the Po completed the line of demarcation to the west; while on the south Fiume gave access to the Adriatic and the line of the Save and Drave rivers eastwards to Belgrade provided a workable frontier to the Ottoman empire. The ruler of this irregular quadrilateral held alike the chief accesses from east to west and west to east, and controlled through Lombardy, Tyrol, Carinthia, and Carniola, the chief and most accessible routes from the centre and north of Germany to the south and the Mediterranean. Geography therefore, perhaps more than anything else, had made 'Austria' a political necessity and held together the areas inhabited by different races. But it had also imposed a cruel dilemma. Did the future of 'Austria' lie to the east or to the west, in concentrating or becoming more and more a German state of central Europe, or a south-eastern state whose line of development lay along the Danube and down the valley of the Morava from Belgrade to Salonica, and whose mission was to unify and amalgamate with the centre the Slav races? Could she nationalize and unify Germany under her control—make the imperial title and power a reality—or should she make herself the heir of the Ottoman empire and unify the Balkans? The history of 'Austria' from 1713 to 1867 suggests that she tried, sometimes successively, sometimes simultaneously, both policies, and failed in both. In 1718 she had acquired the Banat of Temesvar with Belgrade, Orsova, and Craiova; but in 1739 she was compelled to restore Belgrade, Orsova, and Craiova, and retain the Banat. By 1763 Silesia—the bastion to the north of Bohemia—had been definitively ceded to Prussia. The efforts to add Bavaria (between 1778 and 1786), or to exchange the Austrian Netherlands for Bavaria, broke down, and Austria's sole acquisition was the Quarter of the Inn (Innviertel). On the other hand, she had added the county of Zips (1770), the Bukowina (1777), and Galicia (with Lodomeria) in 1772. The third partition of Poland in 1795 gave her another large slice of Polish territory (West or New Galicia—see Plate XXVII). Her defeat, however, in the Three Coalitions (1792–1805) against Revolutionary and Napoleonic France involved momentous and damaging results. In 1797 (Peace of Campo Formio) she abandoned the Netherlands, Falkenstein, the Breisgau, Milan, and Mantua; in return she obtained Venetia proper and Venetian Dalmatia. In 1801 (Peace of Lunéville) she lost Ortenau and all her possessions west of the Rhine, and Tuscany (exchanged for Salzburg), to receive in return the secularized bishoprics of Trent and Brixen. In 1805 (Treaty of Presburg) she lost Venetia and Venetian Dalmatia, Goritz, and Gradisca, Voralberg, and Tyrol with Trent and Brixen. Finally, in 1809 the Treaty of Vienna, which ended the war of that year, brought Austria to her nadir. The Inn Quarter and most of Salzburg were ceded to Bavaria, New Galicia was added to the Napoleonic grand-duchy of Warsaw, Tarnopol given to Russia, while France carved the Illyrian provinces out of the Austrian possessions in Istria, Carniola, Carinthia, and Croatia. Austria was reduced to a purely inland state, not touching the sea at any point, and retaining only Bohemia, Moravia, Hungary, Transylvania, Galicia, the arch-duchy of Austria, Styria, part of Croatia and Slavonia. Furthermore, the dissolution of the Holy Roman empire in 1806, and the formation of the Confederation of the Rhine, had thrust her out of all share in the organization and political life of Napoleonic Germany. The assumption of the title of 'Emperor of Austria' in 1806, coincident with these rapid changes, registered a revolution in the position of Austria, and the opening of a new chapter in Habsburg history.

The reconstitution of 1815 is profoundly significant of Austrian policy as shaped by Metternich. Austria made no effort to reclaim and recover the vulnerable possessions in Germany and the Low

Countries. The Austria of 1815 is a state built up round the middle Danube and controlling north Italy and the northern Adriatic. To the recovery of Voralberg, Tyrol, and the Illyrian provinces, lost in 1809, were added Lombardy and Venetia with Trieste and Istria. For the first time in the history of his house the Habsburg emperor ruled over a state geographically compact, but the settlement of 1815 did not solve the dilemma that the geographical position and racial diversity continuously imposed on statesmanship at Vienna. The collective diplomacy of the Great Powers had furthermore, by the Treaties of 1815, only thwarted, diverted, or damped down the forces of nationality and democracy. From 1815 to 1848 Austria was given thirty years of peace in which to solve the problem of her internal and financial reorganization, and to convert the diplomatic effort at geographical solidarity into a real political unity and organization in which Italian, Slav, Teuton, Magyar, and Roumanian might have achieved a federal centralization (based on provincial autonomy), transcending racial, religious, and territorial schisms and providing a framework for a combined development of the best in each racial group. The Revolution of 1848 and the reaction of 1849-50 only revealed that Metternich and his successors were the discredited protagonists of a worn-out creed. Half a century had been wasted in maintaining a *status quo* which had never really existed, except on the paper of treaties or in the superstitions of statesmen. In 1859 Austria had to cede Lombardy to a new and nationalist Italy, and the Habsburg ' settlements 'in Tuscany, Modena, and Parma and the sphere of influence in Naples vanished like ghosts in the night. The war of 1866 shattered Austrian predominance in the German Confederation and thrust Austria a second time out of Germany altogether, as well as completed the unification of Italy by the cession of Venetia. The ' Compromise ' (*Ausgleich*) of 1867 created indeed the dual monarchy of Austria-Hungary, but it did not solve the problems of internal government and of foreign policy. Expansion to the west and north was blocked by nationalist states—Germany, Russia, Italy. Expansion to the south-east could indeed be made at the expense of a dying Ottoman empire, but the old programme and policy of conquest were too late in 1867. The forces of racial autonomy and nationalism, which had wrested Italy and Germany from Habsburg control, and were vivified by the events of 1848-70, had transformed the whole Balkan question and recreated the Balkan peoples. Only a state armed with the driving moral power derived from internal cohesion and political solidarity and inspired with sympathy for the aspirations of the Slav races within and without its frontiers (and at least 40 per cent. of Austrian subjects belonged to one or other branch of the Slav race) could have achieved success. The occupation of Bosnia and Herzegovina in 1878, authorized by the Treaty of Berlin, and converted into annexation in 1908, was a challenge to Europe and the Balkan kingdoms ; for it threatened to destroy both the achievements of the past and the future evolution of the Near East. The answer to the ' ultimatum ' of 1908 can most easily be grasped by a brief review of the history of the Ottoman empire in Europe, revealed in Plates XXII-XXVI.

Constantinople fell to the Turks in 1453, but Ottoman power in Europe did not reach its zenith until the end of the sixteenth century, when all Hungary (save a strip west of Komorn and the river Raab), Transylvania, Bukowina, Bessarabia, the Danubian provinces of Moldavia and Wallachia, modern Bosnia, Serbia, the Balkan peninsula, Greece, and Morea, and most of the Aegean Islands were in Turkish hands or Turkish tributaries. The Black Sea was virtually a Turkish lake, and the Turkish fleet in the eastern Mediterranean, despite the great defeat at Lepanto (1572), was a formidable power. Crete was conquered as late as 1669, and Podolia in 1672, but the failure of the great assault on Vienna in 1683 and the loss of Buda Pesth in 1686 mark the commencement of the ebbing of the Turkish tide : and from that date until 1789 the Turkish frontier was pushed slowly back.

Until the middle of the eighteenth century the House of Austria was Turkey's most serious foe. In 1699 the Habsburgs had recovered Hungary (with the exception of Temesvar between the rivers Theiss and Maros), Transylvania, and much of Slavonia and Croatia ; in 1718 Temesvar and Craiova, with Belgrade and north Bosnia, were added ; but in 1739 Craiova, with Orsova and Belgrade, was won back by the Turks. She also recovered the Peloponnese from Venice, which had held it from 1699-1718, though the Ionian Islands remained in Venetian possession.

By 1770 the second great European competitor—Russia—for the heritage of Turkey, had definitely appeared on the scene. To Russia, as the great Slav power and the champion of the Greek Orthodox Church, Constantinople was more than the Mecca of her Church—it meant the freedom of the Black Sea and the entrance to the warm waters of the eastern Mediterranean. If Petrograd had been Peter the Great's ' window into Europe ', Constantinople was the door to sea-power and equality of opportunity in the west. Both for Austria and Russia the fate of Turkey was inextricably bound up with the fate of Poland. (See Plates XXVII and XXIX.) For in the eyes of eighteenth-century statesmen the Eastern question was as much a Polish as a Turkish problem. In 1772 the first partition of Poland foreshadowed the final dismemberment of the kingdom, whose sovereign had saved Vienna in 1683. In 1774 the Treaty of Kutchuk Kanardji made the Crimea independent of Turkish suzerainty (it was annexed to Russia in 1784), ceded Azov and the right of free navigation to Russian ships in the Black Sea. Russia had thus acquired a firm footing on the northern littoral of the Black Sea and something far more important for the future, a treaty-right of making representations on behalf of the Greek Church in the Ottoman empire, and of the Roumanian Danubian principalities of Moldavia and Wallachia, i. e. the right to intervene in the internal affairs and administration of the Turkish dominions.

By 1800 events had marched fast. Austria acquired the Bukowina in 1777, and Orsova in 1790 ; in 1792 the Peace of Jassy moved the Russian frontier to the Dniester. By 1796 the buffer state of Poland had ceased to exist, and the Russian boundary now marched with both Prussia and Austria from the Niemen to the Carpathians. The establishment of a Russian consulate at Bucharest was significant—Russia was claiming to be the protector of the Christian subjects of the Sublime Porte. In the west Austria in 1797 acquired the Dalmatian territories of Venice, and thereby encircled Bosnia, while the Ionian Islands were set up as an independent republic under the joint protection of Russia and Turkey. The modern phase of the Turkish question had practically begun. The fate and future of Turkey were no longer a matter for the two Powers geographically most closely connected with the Balkan peninsula ; France was no less deeply interested, and every advance made by Great Britain in the development of British power in India strengthened her anxiety about the political control of routes and communications from west to east and her interest in the eastern Mediterranean, Egypt, the Red Sea, Persian Gulf, and Indian Ocean. The fate of Turkey in Europe could not be separated from the fate of Turkey in Asia. Already in 1791 the problems that constituted the Near Eastern question for the nineteenth century were beginning to combine into a formidable whole—(1) the special interests and ambitions of separate states such as Austria or Russia, whose further expansion could only be effected by the absorption of Turkish territory ; (2) the demand for liberation from Turkish rule of subject national groups—Serb, Bulgar, Greek, Roumanian ; (3) the intervention of the great European states, directly or indirectly interested in the future of these groups or opposed to the aggrandizement of Austria or Russia. The Turk, it was already said, was sick and dying—his expulsion from Europe had been demanded by Burke in England in 1791. Was the ' sick man ' to be allowed to die a natural death from internal sepsis and decay, and his heritage left to accident or a crafty opportunism, or to be compelled to commit emicide, or to be put out of existence by a surgical operation of the combined chancelleries of Europe, which would then incorporate the inheritance by agreement ? Within the Turkish dominions the problem was one of conflicting nationalities, races, religions, and historic traditions ; but Europe had still to decide in a choice of evils whether the maintenance of the integrity of the Turkish dominions was not a preferable solution to partition, aggravated by European war. Did the future lie with dismemberment by forces without, or the revolt of forces within, the Turkish empire ?

The failure of Napoleon's Eastern policy and dreams is recorded in the silence of the map—the Napoleonic epoch only bequeathed a heightened and unsatisfied French interest in the future of Syria and Egypt. The Russian advance continued (Plate XXIX) ; in 1812 the Treaty of Bucharest made the river Pruth the frontier, gave Bessarabia and the delta of the Danube to Russia, and confirmed the Russian right to internal intervention. The settlement of 1815 placed the Ionian Isles under a British protectorate. But the fifteen years between 1815 and 1830 witnessed a remarkable transformation, due mainly to revolt from within and the renaissance of racial and nationalist ambitions and ideals whose roots lay in ancient history, forgotten by or unknown to Europe, but an imperishable memory to the races for four centuries submerged beneath the Turkish flood. The Serb remembered the greater Serbia of Tsar Stephen Dushan, shattered at Kossovopolje, ' The Field of Blackbirds' (1389); the Bulgar remembered the Bulgarian kingdom of Tsar Samuel (923–34) and of Tsar Simon (976–1014); the Greek the greater classical Greece that had held and civilized both European and Asiatic shores of the Aegean and had made the mediaeval Greek empire of the East ; the Roumanian that Moldavia, Wallachia, Bessarabia, and Transylvania, separated by political but anti-national frontiers, were inhabited by a preponderant population of kindred race, speech, and religion. It was between 1815 and 1830, then, that the formula ' The Balkans not for Austrian or Russian, but for the Balkan peoples ' came to the birth, and events fostered its growth. In 1817 the principality of Serbia emerged on a limited scale and obtained a limited autonomy under Turkish suzerainty. The year 1822 saw the end of Greek Phanariot rule in Moldavia and Wallachia, and the Danubian provinces made tributary to the Turk but administered under native hospodars. In 1830 the Greek War of Independence ended in the establishment of an independent kingdom of Greece —the first independent state created out of Turkish dominions. Russia, too, had not ceased to advance. The Treaty of Adrianople (1829) proclaimed the Black Sea, the Bosphorus, and the Dardanelles free to Russian vessels, riveted Russian control on the Danube delta, and practically made Wallachia and Moldavia a Russian protectorate, while it confirmed the privileges of autonomous Serbia. In the west the little principality of Montenegro, which had never, even in the darkest days, lost its rocky independence, continued its struggle alike against Austrian or Albanian or Turkish (Bosniak) encroachment. War makes strange bedfellows, and the Crimean War of 1854 brought to Turkey Great Britain and France as allies, determined to maintain the integrity of the Ottoman empire against Russian advance. The Treaty of Paris in 1856 pushed back the Russian frontier. Russia ceded part of southern Bessarabia to Moldavia, and the Danubian delta, which was placed under an international commission. The navigation of the Danube and the Black Sea was declared free, while the waters and ports of the latter were closed to the navies of Russia or any other European Power. The signatories promised ' to respect the independence and territorial integrity of the Ottoman empire ', and a series of clauses provided for a liberal programme of internal reform, redressing the grievances of the Christian subjects of the Porte. The ' sick man ', in short, was to be cured by the western pharmacopoeia of the European Concert and maintained in a healthy integrity for the benefit of all, within and without his dominions. The sequel proved that ' the sick man ' would either remain well in his own

Oriental way—Eastern health is frequently disease or lunacy in Western eyes—or remain as sick and as intact as his subjects or the European Powers would allow him to be. In 1859 Moldavia and Wallachia, despite the European Powers, united into a single principality, and in 1866 elected Prince Charles of Hohenzollern-Sigmaringen to be their ruler, the second and not the last German sovereign introduced into the Balkans. Greece, the frontiers of which in 1832 had been advanced from the Gulf of Arta to the Gulf of Volo, received in 1864 the Ionian Isles from Great Britain. A brief peace, and then the volcanic forces beneath the surface exploded. From 1873–6 a series of revolts against Turkish misrule in the Balkans precipitated the Russo-Turkish War of 1877, which brought the Russian army to the door of Constantinople and the British fleet into the Sea of Marmora. Russia in 1871 had already denounced the shackles imposed on her in 1856—a denunciation meekly accepted by the Conference of London (March 13, 1871) —but the Treaties of Berlin (1878) revised or annulled the Treaty of San Stefano and substituted a wholly different settlement under European guarantees. The political principles of this famous settlement are difficult to discover and justify. The independence of Montenegro, Serbia, and Roumania was recognized, and all three received enough territorial expansion to disappoint, though not enough to satisfy, legitimate national aspirations. The map shows (Plates XXIV and XXV) the proposed arrangement contemplated by the Treaty of San Stefano, and revised by the Treaties of Berlin. A tributary and limited Bulgaria was created between the Danube and the Balkans, but the Bulgaria of the Bulgars was thereby cut in half by the retention of eastern Roumelia within the Turkish empire. Three of the great European states (besides Russia) played an important part in the settlement of the Berlin Treaties : (1) Germany under Bismarck disclaimed a direct interest ; (2) Great Britain steadfastly opposed Russia, championed the integrity, so far as possible, of Turkish territories, and claimed to have ' consolidated ' the Ottoman empire. In return for the British promise to defend Turkey and for repeated Turkish promises to introduce reforms, the administration of Cyprus was assigned to Great Britain ; (3) Austria was as hostile to all arrangements that barred her ultimate advance to Salonica by the establishment of independent principalities between her southern frontier and the Aegean as to the aggrandizement of Russian power in the Balkans. By the administrative occupation of Bosnia and Herzegovina she successfully split the solidarity of the southern Slav race, vetoed for thirty years Serbian ambitions, and by her retention of Cattaro put a tourniquet on Montenegrin expansion, although in 1880 Dulcigno was assigned to her as a sop for frustrated hopes. The recovery by Russia of the Bessarabia ceded in 1856, was a sore disappointment to Roumania, compelled to accept as her compensation the malarious Dobrudja and the Danubian delta, which were not in any sense ' Roumanian '. Greece obtained no compensation until 1881, when she acquired Thessaly and part of Epirus—the same year that saw Roumania converted from a principality into a kingdom. Crete, whose union with Greece was demanded both by Greeks and Cretans, still remained Turkish, and a problem both to the Porte and the Concert of Europe.

The Treaties of Berlin are a landmark in Balkan history—only in the sense that they closed one great chapter and opened another no less momentous. The map of 1914 (Plate XXV) is eloquent of fundamental changes which leave the Treaties of 1878 in shreds and tatters ; it is silent on the two impressive facts which underlie the history of the thirty-five years after 1878 : (a) The impotence of the Concert of Europe to achieve its will, when it had one. Failure in the regimen of the Powers has not led to the alteration of the prescription ; it has only meant that the prescription has been re-written, and the doses doubled without any provision for supplying the medicine or compelling the sick patient to take it. (b) Since 1878, and particularly since 1890, the Germany which was ' the honest broker ' of the Berlin

Congress has passed from benevolent passivity to an organized protection, and made the Turkish empire both in Europe and in Asia its special sphere of influence and commercial penetration. The most formidable force behind the Porte has not been the Concert of Europe, but a unified Germany exploiting the commercial resources and utilizing the political and military strength of a reorganized Turkey under German direction to make the framework of the Teutonic empire from Hamburg to Bagdad and the Persian Gulf—a Germany, allied since 1879 with Austria-Hungary, whose policy both within and without her borders rested on the division, denationalization, and subjection of the Slav races, in the interests of the two politically dominant races of the Dual monarchy—the German and the Magyar.

In 1885 eastern Roumelia revolted and united with the Bulgaria of 1878—a union reluctantly recognized by the Powers and the Porte. In 1897 the Greco-Turkish War ended in trifling frontier rectifications in favour of Turkey, and in 1898 Crete was granted, not incorporation with Greece, but autonomy under Turkish suzerainty and European supervision. Ten years later the annexation of Bosnia and Herzegovina by Austria (1908) was followed by Bulgaria's renunciation of Turkish suzerainty and the assumption of the title of Tsar by her Prince, and the formation of the Balkan League of Montenegro, Serbia, Bulgaria, and Greece (1912), which promptly challenged a weakened Turkey, just freed from the war with Italy and the loss of the Tripolitana (October 18, 1912). Completely defeated, the Porte ceded to the Balkan allies all her territory north of the Enos-Midia line, together with Crete—the settlement of Albania, the Aegean islands, and Mount Athos being reserved for the Great Powers (Treaty of London, May 17–30, 1913). The second Balkan War, consequent on the failure of the Balkan allies to agree on the division of the ceded territories, put Serbia, Montenegro, and Greece into the field against Bulgaria, whose defeat was made decisive by the intervention of Roumania. By the Treaty of Bucharest (August 10, 1913) Serbia obtained the eastern half of Novibazar, Kossovo, and Central Macedonia; Montenegro the western half of Novibazar; Greece obtained Epirus, southern Macedonia, Salonica, and the seaboard as far east as Kavala, while Crete proclaimed its union with Greece; Bulgaria secured part of western Thrace, the upper Struma and Mesta valleys, but was obliged to cede to Roumania a strip of territory between the Danube and the Black Sea. Turkey had taken advantage of the second Balkan War to reoccupy Adrianople, in defiance of the Treaty of London, and as Bulgaria was unable and the Concert of Europe unwilling to compel her by force to withdraw, she retained what she had seized. The delimitation of an autonomous Albania was accomplished by the end of 1913, when the crown was accepted by Prince Frederick William of Wied (February 21, 1914), only to be resigned in September of the same year, leaving Albania's future an unsettled riddle.

Apart from the problems raised by the great European War, two conclusions are suggested by the events of 1912–14 and the settlements of London and Bucharest: (1) The rupture of the Balkan alliance and the terms of the Treaty of Bucharest are not the last word in the problem of satisfying the aspirations of the Balkan peoples. (2) The defeat of Turkey was also a defeat of Austria and Austrian policy since 1878. If for no other reason, 'unredeemed Serbia' and 'unredeemed Roumania', the anomalous position of Albania, the unsettled question of the Aegean islands, and the continuance of the Turk at Constantinople, point to the truth of A. Sorel's remark: 'On the day when the Eastern Question appears to have been solved, Europe will inevitably be confronted with the Austrian Question.'

Plate XXVI. The Ottoman empire in Asia has suffered fewer territorial losses than the African and European portions of the Turkish dominions. In Europe and Africa, as has been seen, the shrinkage has been both continuous and severe, but in Asia since the eighteenth century, with the exception of the Russian advance in the Caucasus, some trifling concessions on the Persian frontier,

and the complete failure to master Arabia, the Turk still is practically ruler in 1914 where he was ruler in 1789. The fate of the islands off the coast of Asia Minor in the Aegean, largely Greek in population, had not been finally decided when the Treaty of Lausanne (October 18, 1912) ended the Turco-Italian war and the Treaties of London and Bucharest ended the two Balkan wars; Cyprus had been leased to Great Britain by the Convention of June 4, 1878, confirmed by the Treaty of Berlin, but otherwise the map of Asiatic Turkey provides no startling transfers of territory. Asiatic Turkey has on its eastern frontier Russia and Persia, to the west the Khedivate of Egypt (the frontier line running from Akaba at the head of the Gulf of that name to the port of Rafa on the Mediterranean), and to the south independent Arabia, where Turkish territory is limited to the strip of El Hasa, on the western shore of the Persian Gulf, and to the vilayets of Hejaz and Yemen, which include the holy cities of Medina and Mecca, stretching along the eastern shore of the Red Sea and bounded by the frontier of the British Protectorate of Aden, extended and delimited in 1901–2. Geographically as well as politically this Asiatic empire which connects eastern Europe with western Asia and which is washed by the Black Sea, Aegean, Mediterranean, Red Sea, and Persian Gulf, is composed of five fairly well marked divisions—Anatolia or Asia Minor proper, the Armenian and Kurdish highlands, Mesopotamia (the fertile alluvial lowlands of the basins of the Tigris and Euphrates rivers), the provinces of Syria and Palestine separated from Mesopotamia by the Syrian desert, and the Arabian coast-lands. In Syria alone Europe has effectively intervened. In the Lebanon district, where the Maronite Christians are the dominant part of the population, and as a consequence of the sanguinary massacres by the Turks and Druses in combination, which led to French intervention under Napoleon III, the Convention of the Lebanon provided (1861 and 1864) that henceforth there should be a Christian governor, with the title of Grand Vizier, and appointed by the Ottoman Government, for the Sanjak or administrative areas as delineated in the document. This règlement organique was guaranteed by the signatory Great Powers, who forced it upon the Sublime Porte in the interests of an oppressed Christian population, anxious only to retain its religious freedom.

The future of Asiatic Turkey is more important than its immediate past or present. It is the true core of Turkish power, and the steady shrinkage of Turkey in Europe and Africa only emphasizes the conclusion that their Asiatic dominions are the true home of the Turk, where, judged by racial and religious tests, he probably outnumbers all the non-Turkish and non-Mohammedan groups reckoned together. But, unless the experiences and events of a century are wholly misleading, significant modifications are indicated in the future. Armenia, at the mercy alike of Turk and Kurd, imperatively demands similar treatment to that of the Lebanon district. The steady Greek infiltration into the eastern littoral of the Aegean, and the character of the islands, constitute strong claims for an expanding Greece. Northern and central Arabia under their Wahabite rulers have successfully repulsed the efforts of the Turks and of ambitious Egyptian Pashas, such as Mehemet Ali between 1811 and 1840, to destroy their independence. The sheikhs and chiefs of the Hadramaut between the Aden Protectorate at the south-western corner (with its hold on the islands of Perim and Socotra) and the frontiers of the Sultanate of Oman, have been brought under a British Protectorate, which shields them from Bedouin and Wahabite alike; and from Muscat to the Turkish strip of El Hasa on the Persian Gulf—the Pirate coast—the chiefs have found that a de facto British Protectorate is as satisfactory a form of political control as political control to the anarchy of independent piracy can be. Further north the Sheikh of Koweit, the most important natural harbour in the Gulf, in 1899, in order to repel a Turkish effort to assert authority never more than nominal and lapsed from inability to enforce it, placed himself under British protection and thereby checkmated the plan of securing, in defiance of British warnings and without British consent, a Turco-German terminus for the Bagdad Railway.

If the Turk in Europe has been a grave danger to the European states, the European states are now proving a grave danger to the Turk in Asia. For the Turk possesses territories which, if he is not strong enough to hold against all, are too valuable strategically and economically to be disposed of to a European state, ready to protect him in return for a free hand and a monopoly of exploitation. And the reasons are plain. They are military, economic, political, and religious. Turkey in Asia provides the easiest route for connecting the Asiatic empire of two European powers—Great Britain and Russia—with direct access by land to the Mediterranean at half a dozen points. But as economic exploitation in hostile hands means military vulnerability for those against whom it is aimed, all Turkish railway concessions become suspicious in inverse proportion to their apparent innocence. Secondly, it is Turkey in Asia no less than Turkey in Europe which by its mastery of the Bosphorus and the Dardanelles shuts out the Russian empire from the Aegean and the Mediterranean. A Turkish empire that accepts the destiny of being a German automaton is not merely a menace to the Balkan peoples, but to the whole European state system. Thirdly, the future of the Turk is bound up with the future of Islamism, which is a matter of the deepest concern to France, to Russia, and, above all, to Great Britain. Neither the German nor the Austrian empires are Mohammedan powers. The experience of the last twenty years has proved that sacrifices of Armenian, Jew, or Greek to Mohammedan fanaticism, combined with the exploitation of Islamism in the political and commercial interests of a non-Mohammedan empire, are the one solution of the Turkish problem both in Asia and in Europe which is incompatible with the peace of the world or the continued existence of a Turkish empire.

Plates XXVII and XXVIII. A diplomatist of the middle of the eighteenth century, confronted with the map of eastern and south-eastern Europe in 1914, would pause over one momentous fact—the disappearance of the kingdom of Poland, which had figured in European politics as a powerful monarchy since 1295, though the title of King had been claimed by its rulers at least two hundred years earlier. The Poland of the seventeenth and eighteenth centuries was the result of the Union of Lublin (1569), which united, under an elective monarchy, Lithuania and Poland proper into a vast state whose frontiers stretched from the Baltic Sea in the north to the Black Sea in the south. Holding Livonia, Courland, Lithuania, Ermeland, and West Prussia (the duchy of East Prussia was a fief of the Teutonic Order under Polish suzerainty), Poland was the greatest of the Baltic powers in the sixteenth century; in central and eastern Europe she controlled the great Vistula river almost from its source in the Moravian mountains to its mouth at Danzig, and her ancient capital at Cracow blocked the strategic entrance and exit by the Moravian Gate; to the south the solid barrier of the Carpathians gave her Galicia and Lodomeria, and thence she stretched down the Dniester to the Black Sea, holding Podolia, the Ukraine, and the Cossacks of the Dnieper in varying degrees of dependence, very difficult to define. The vast size and territorial continuity of this dual kingdom of Poland-Lithuania made it formidable and promised a future of incalculable potency if it could be welded into an efficient unity. But its character and position contained four fatal flaws: (1) The elective character of the monarchy prevented continuity of policy and made the Polish crown, after 1572, when the last of the Jagellon dynasty died, a prize for intrigue, ambition, and corruption alike to foreign rulers and the native aristocracy, and the kingdom the battleground of foreign states striving to secure the control of eastern Europe. (2) It was not racially compact, for it consisted broadly of

three different races—Poles, Lithuanians, and Russians—the Little Russians or Ruthenes of Eastern Galicia, Lodomeria, Kieff, and the Dnieper, and the White Russians of the area north of the marshes of the Pripet, both groups racially and linguistically akin to the Great Russians of Moscow and Novgorod. Of the population of the Poland of 1569 probably not more than one-third were Poles proper. Moreover, in West and East Prussia and Livonia the influence and infiltration of the German race and civilization were steadily progressing. (3) The Poland of 1569 had consolidated itself, while its neighbours—the German and the Scandinavian in the west, and the Slav states to the east—were either still being remade in the crucible of the Reformation or had not yet emerged from the struggle with Tartar invasions. But from 1600 onwards Poland had to deal with a strong and united Sweden bent on supremacy in the Baltic, with a Prussia becoming conscious of its future, with the great House of Austria, with a waning Turkish empire, and from 1613 onwards with the House of Romanov, painfully but unceasingly building up the framework of a Russian state at Moscow, on the foundation laid by Ivan the Third. (4) Geography had denied Poland either natural boundaries or defensible frontiers. Unless the Polish monarchy could be more efficient than its rivals and neighbours, and more capable of organized effort and the vision that dreams ahead for the future and can plan in the present the framework for the dreams to grow into and take shape, the kingdom of Poland-Lithuania, vast, shapeless, unwieldy, and lacking racial homogeneity, was bound to become an inexhaustible Naboth's vineyard if Ahaba grew up and flourished on every frontier. From 1572, however, Poland grew less and less efficient; her last great king was John Sobieski (1673–96), who saved Vienna from the Turks (1683), and who had harder struggles to fight with his selfish, turbulent, and anarchic nobility than with Turk, Slav, or German. By 1621 Sweden had conquered Esthonia and Livonia. In 1660 the Elector of Brandenburg wrested East Prussia from Polish suzerainty. In 1672 Poland ceded Podolia to the Turks. In 1667 she surrendered Smolensk and waived, in favour of Russia, her suzerainty over the Cossack republic of Zaporogia, in revolt from Polish authority.

The Poland of the eighteenth century had two formidable foes—the Russian empire as Peter the Great had left it, and the kingdom of Prussia, not because it was big, but because since the Great Elector (1640–88) its rulers were hammering a state together by administrative ability and the patience that is ruthless. Sweden had gone down (see Plate XXXI); the House of Austria was involved in the south-east and with the effort to maintain a challenged supremacy in central Germany; Turkey was useless as an ally and menaced by the same dangers as Poland herself. The elective monarchy and the Polish nobility —manipulated and willing to be manipulated—condemned the kingdom to disunion, impoverishment, and impotence. Fate, moreover, decreed that the ablest of the Hohenzollerns, Frederick the Great (1740–86), should coincide with the ablest successor of Peter the Great, Catherine (1762–97), the German woman who made her policy the embodiment of Slav ambitions and dreams. An independent or a strong Poland vetoed alike the consolidation of Prussia and the advance of a consolidated Russia into the heart of the European state-system. Frederick and Catherine sealed the fate of Poland and made the House of Austria, without difficulty, an accomplice in the decision. When Poland would have cured by reforms the maladies that made her vulnerable and impotent, it was too late. Neither Prussia nor Austria, and least of all Russia, desired a reformed and a strong Poland.

The three partitions of 1772, 1793, and 1795 obliterated from the map one of the ancient monarchies of Europe. Russia acquired in 1772 Polish Livonia, and the territory to the east of the Düna-Dnieper, whilst Prussia obtained West Prussia and Ermeland (but without Danzig), and Austria obtained Galicia and Lodomeria. In 1793 Russia annexed Podolia and the Ukraine, with parts of Volhynia and Podolia, and in 1795 Courland and Samogitia, the remainder of Podolia and Volhynia with Lithuania east of the Niemen. In 1793 Prussia took Danzig and Thorn, most of Great Poland and Cujavia, and part of Masovia, Austria not participating in this partition. Finally, in 1795, the remainder of Poland was divided between Austria and Prussia, the former securing Cracow, the latter Warsaw. It is noticeable that Russia, by incorporating Lithuania, together with the areas of White and Little Russia, had not acquired Polish-speaking territories —the Russian gains added the non-Russian Lithuanians and Russian areas kindred in race and speech to the great Russia of Petrograd, Moscow, and Novgorod. Austria had in eastern Galicia split the racial unity of the Ruthenes or Little Russians, but the Poland of the Poles was dismembered between Prussia and Austria, thereby bringing a great influx of the Slav element into both states and dividing a race, one in its language, literature, blood, and religion, between two German monarchies. The partitions practically recreated the spirit of Polish nationality, and Napoleon's grand duchy of Warsaw, constituted between 1806 and 1810, was an attempt to weaken both Prussia and Austria by establishing a resurrected if diminished Poland on the flanks of both monarchies, and by setting up a buffer state under French protection between Russia and Europe. It was constituted by welding together broadly the Prussian and Austrian shares in the partitions of 1793 and 1795, together with eastern Galicia and with Warsaw as the capital of the duchy.

The reconstitution of Poland was one of the most critical problems of the Congress at Vienna 1814-15. The Tsar Alexander I desired to create under Russian suzerainty an autonomous Polish state which would have included the whole of the Napoleonic grand duchy. In return, Prussia would annex the whole of the kingdom of Saxony. Russia and Prussia were both willing to accept this arrangement—which would have brought the Polish and Russian frontier within ninety miles of Berlin—and it is not the least of the ironies of history that British and French opposition to it, combining with Austrian fear of Russia, caused it to be so substantially modified as to establish a wholly different settlement. A kingdom of Poland was indeed set up under Russian suzerainty, but it was a very diminished Poland. Prussia retained Thorn and Danzig and the modern province of Posen (Posnania), thereby pushing back the Russo-Polish frontier to a distance of 180 miles from Berlin; Austria recovered eastern Galicia, and Cracow with a strip of territory was established as an independent republic. The results, therefore, of the eighteenth-century partitions—the dismemberment of the Polish race under three states, Russia, Prussia, and Austria—were maintained. The autonomy of Russian Poland of 1815 continued until the Polish Revolution of 1831, on the failure of which the constitution granted in 1815 was withdrawn and Poland was incorporated with Russia. Strictly speaking, Poland does not exist, for the Russian Poles are distributed in the ten Russian provinces or governments of the Vistula. With the exception of the suppression in 1846 of the free republic of Cracow and its annexation by Austria, no change has been made in the territorial boundaries laid down in 1815—one of the rare instances in which the frontiers fixed by the Treaties of Vienna have lasted for a whole century. A reconstitution of Poland on nationalist lines would involve a drastic reconstitution of the eastern frontier of Austria and the German empire. There are probably 11 millions of Poles in the provinces of the Vistula; but there are also probably at least 3½ millions in Prussia and 4½ millions in Austria. 'Unredeemed' Poland has to be added to the problems which the statesmanship of the twentieth century cannot evade, but the solution of which is only easy on paper and on maps that conceal the political difficulties.

Plates XXIX, XXX, and XXXI have a common subject-matter— for if they are not solely concerned with the political development and geographical evolution of Russia as a European state,

unquestionably Russia is their central theme, round which other developments are most naturally grouped. The central core of the Russian state which emerged in the seventeenth century was a union of Slav principalities, kindred in race, language, and religion, the chiefs of which were the princes of Moscow, Smolensk, Kieff, and Novgorod, ruling over subjects— the Great Russians (as distinct from the Ruthenes or Little Russians in the south and south-west) of the vast plain, intersected by great rivers, which stretches from the basin of the Oder and the Vistula to the Ural mountains and is continued into the modern Siberia. But geography, in constituting this vast area with natural frontiers in the hills and thousand lakes of Finland, the Oder, the Netze, the Bohemian and Moravian mountains, the Carpathians, the Black Sea, the Caucasus, the Caspian, and the Urals, had provided a gigantic matrix for a state of inexhaustible possibilities, which must inevitably develop very slowly; and the dawn of modern history brought into this huge and irregular quadrilateral the branches of the Slav race to multiply and become as the sands of the sea for multitude. History and geography had also linked the area with Asia; hence the first great obstacle to Russian union was the invasion and foreign dominion of Mongols and Tartars pressing westwards. The break-up of the Golden Horde in 1489 from a single khanate, whose capital was Sarai on the Volga, into several khanates, gave the princes of Moscow their opportunity, and Ivan III (1462-1505) made Moscow the centre of a Russian union, which brought Novgorod, Tver, Viatka, and Chernigov under his rule and established his independence of the Tartar khans. The Russian state was born, and from Ivan's marriage with Sophia Palaeologa, niece of the last Greek emperor of Constantinople, dates the assumption of the imperial double-headed Eagle of the Caesars and the title of Tsar. Henceforward Tsars ruling in Moscow might claim a double historic mission—to unite and be the Tsar of all the Russias, Great, Small, Black, White, and Red (names derived from the titles in mediaeval maps of the branches of the Russian races), and to recover from the Turk the capital of the former Greek eastern empire, whence had come in the tenth century the conversion of the Russians to the Greek orthodox branch of the Christian church. In the east it was not difficult for Russia to expand and become the successor of the Mongol khanate, but in the west the way was blocked by the Ottoman empire, the duchy of Lithuania united since 1569 with the kingdom of Poland, with the German militant Orders of the Sword and of the Teutonic Knights which had penetrated East Prussia, Courland, and Livonia, and secured a strong footing on the Baltic, and with the Scandinavian states, Sweden above all. The struggle was not merely one for territory and strategic positions, but of conflicting races, religions, languages, and civilizations. The Swedes were Scandinavian and Protestant; the Poles were Slav but Roman Catholic; the Lithuanians were of an Aryan race (Lithuanians proper, Letts, and Esthonians), distinct alike from Slav, Teuton, or Scandinavian, and partly Catholic, partly Greek in religion; and in the south were the Moslem Turks and the khanates of Kazan, Astrakhan, and the Crimea. But the Muscovite power could only reach western seas by absorption or conquest of those who denied her access.

The process by which Poland-Lithuania was extinguished has already been briefly traced. It remains to mark the stages of Russian advance (a) in the Baltic lands and (b) in the south-east of Europe. (a) The Baltic, after the Mediterranean, is the second great inland European sea, whose importance is based on the lands that make its shores, the commercial resources that soil, climate, and industry have given it, and the geographical configuration which closes it at its western end to the North Sea and the oceans beyond. The struggle for supremacy in the Baltic is a leading characteristic of northern history in the sixteenth and seventeenth centuries. Had the Scandinavian kingdom of Denmark (with Norway) and Sweden been able to unite, the

Baltic would have become and might have remained a Scandinavian lake ; but the fatal disunion of these kindred states condemned in the sequel both Denmark and Sweden to a second-rate position, and on the ruins of Scandinavian disunion was built up Prussian and Russian power. In 1697 Sweden held Finland, Ingrelia, Carelia, and Livonia, western Pomerania, and the duchies of Bremen and Verden. The anti-Swedish League of Hanover, Denmark, Prussia, Poland, and Russia brought the Swedish empire down, and Peter the Great, by the Treaty of Nystad (1721), not only secured his ' window into Europe ' at Petrograd, but the Swedish provinces of Ingrelia, Carelia, and Livonia, and parts of Kexholm and Viborg in Finland. Prussia ousted Sweden from Stettin and the mouth of the Oder, Hanover secured Bremen and Verden. In 1743 (Peace of Åbo) Finland east of the river Kymmene was ceded to Russia ; and the Polish partition of 1772 gave both Prussia and Russia a firmer footing on the Baltic shore. Thus in 1789 (Plate XXXI) there is a balance of power in the Baltic, shared between Denmark, Sweden, Prussia, and Russia, with Poland maintaining a precarious existence at Danzig—an enclave in German territory—and still nominally master of Courland and Samogitia.

The next changes prove that the future lay with Russia and Prussia, and that the struggle for supremacy in the Baltic would be a struggle of Slav v. Teuton. In 1809 the rest of Finland, with the Åland Islands, was annexed by Alexander I, and the settlement of 1815 restored Danzig to Prussia and awarded her the last remnant of Swedish territory in West Pomerania. If Russia ruled from the Gulf of Bothnia to Memel, Prussia was virtually master of the southern coast from Königsberg to Lübeck, and the winter ice meant that for six months in the year Petrograd lost its access by water to the west. Norway was assigned to Sweden (a union maintained until 1905, when Norway broke the bonds of Vienna and was established as an independent kingdom), and Denmark, which held, through the Sound and the Great Belt, the keys to the Baltic, was a Continental state in virtue of the duchies of Schleswig and Holstein. The Danish war of 1864, which tore Schleswig and Holstein from the Danish monarchy, was the final blow to Scandinavian power and influence in the Baltic ; for with their annexation in 1866, not to the German Confederation, but to Prussia, which at the same time absorbed Hanover, the great outlets both to the Baltic and the North Sea—the river mouths of the Ems, Weser, Elbe, Oder, and Vistula—were in Prussian hands. The magnificent harbour of Kiel was especially desired by the far-seeing Bismarck, for a canal had only to be constructed between it and the mouth of the Elbe and what nature had allotted to Denmark could be annulled without war, annexation, or alliance. With the completion of the Kaiser Wilhelm canal in 1898, and the transfer of Heligoland (guarding the entrance to the Elbe) from Great Britain in 1891, Prussia was able to sail her ships of war from the North Sea to Königsberg at all seasons of the year without political or maritime let or hindrance—a striking example of how the sea, when controlled by sea-power, does not divide but unites. The long struggle for supremacy in the Baltic has seen the rise and fall of Swedish power, the reduction of Denmark, the expansion of Russia—but it has left Prussia, controlling the strength of the Germany she has united under her presidency, master of the situation. For Russia the Baltic remains an inland lake, the exits of which can be as effectively closed against her as are the exits from the Black Sea. From the purely Russian point of view, Russian acquiescence in the overthrowal of Denmark in 1864 was a blunder which her subsequent policy in Finland and the fears it aroused in Scandinavia of a further Russian advance have not corrected. Two agreements (dated April 23, 1908) must be noted here : the first between Germany, Denmark, Russia, and Sweden ; the second between Germany, Denmark, Great Britain, France, the Netherlands, and Sweden, applying respectively to ' the regions which border on the Baltic Sea ' and ' the regions which border

upon the North Sea ', assert the desire of the signatories to maintain the existing *status quo* and the sovereign rights of the countries represented, and in the event of a menace to either, to concert by agreement measures for the maintenance of that *status quo*.

(b) Russian expansion in the south has been no less marked. Azof was conquered in 1696, only to be restored to the Porte in 1711, but in 1774, as already noted, the territory between the Dnieper and the Bug was acquired ; in 1783 the Crimea was annexed ; in 1792 the frontier was advanced to the Dniester, and in 1812 to the Pruth—thereby securing the north-western shores of the Black Sea. The north-eastern and eastern shores were secured by a gradual advance towards the Caucasus and the Caspian. In 1725 the Russian frontier ran in an irregular line from Azof to the river Terek on the Caspian ; by 1815 Kuban (1784), Derbend, and Baku (1806), Georgia, Mingrelia, and Karabagh (1803) had been annexed, so that the western shore of the Caspian as far as the Persian frontier was Russian. The nineteenth century has witnessed a steady progress and consolidation. In 1828 Erivan was ceded by Persia ; the conquest and absorption of Kuban, Circassia, and Daghestan were completed between 1859 and 1864, and though Kars was captured in 1855 its final cession with the free port of Batoum was not made until the Treaty of Berlin of 1878. The southern shore of the Black Sea from Trebizond westwards alone remains in Turkish hands.

The control of the eastern shore of the Caspian has come with the growth of the Russian empire in Asia. Russia indeed was a great Asiatic power before her position in Europe had been definitely consolidated. The eastward sweep of the Cossacks had by 1800 brought the whole of Siberia up to the Chinese frontier under the Tsars. The advance into Turkestan south of the frontier line of 1846 has been the feature of the second half of the nineteenth century, for it has met a similar advance northwest from the Punjab of the British power established in India. The successive stages are clearly shown on Plate XXXII— Tashkend (1865), Samarkand (1868), Khiva, the Amu Daria and Trans-Caspian provinces (1873), Akhal Tekke (1881), Merv (1884), the Pamirs (1895). The Russian frontier therefore runs from the Attrek river on the Caspian, along the northern boundary of Afghanistan to the Pamirs, where it meets the frontier of Chinese Turkestan and of the British north-west frontier province on the Hindu Kush. Half a century of feverish fears and restless advances on both sides was ended by the Anglo-Russian Convention of August 31, 1907. This dealt with three countries—Persia, Afghanistan, and Thibet. (1) Persia. (See Plate XXXIII.) Here both Russia and Great Britain agreed to respect the integrity and independence of the country, which was divided into three zones, a northern recognized as the Russian sphere of influence, a southern as the British, and a central in which the signatory powers pledged themselves to abstain from political interference without previous arrangement with each other and by mutual consent. (2) Afghanistan was recognized as being within the British sphere of influence, and Russia undertook to conduct all negotiations with the Amir through Great Britain as an intermediary. Afghanistan therefore was constituted as a buffer state between the two empires and under British protection. (3) Thibet was recognized as subject to Chinese sovereignty ; its territorial integrity and independence were to be preserved, and both Russia and Great Britain undertook to conduct their negotiations through the Chinese Government.

Furthermore, the recognition by Russia that Great Britain had ' special interests ' in the Persian Gulf emphasizes the importance of that area. Those interests had been built up over two centuries in order to protect trade and the sea and land communications with India. The task of abolishing piracy and slavery, reducing the lawless chiefs whose strongholds were dotted on both shores of the Gulf, of surveying and charting its waters for safe navigation, of enforcing law and order for all, had been steadily pursued since the end of the eighteenth century and entitled Great Britain to claim, as she did in 1903, the Gulf as practically within her sphere of influence and under her protection, and to make it clear that the establishment of a hostile power, threatening commerce and the British dominion in India, within the area of the Gulf could not be permitted. It is noticeable that British power and influence have not been advanced by annexation, but by concluding treaty arrangements with the tribal and territorial chiefs. On the Arabian shore the Katif coast alone is Turkish. The Sultan of Oman, the Sheikhs of Bahrein and Koweit, and the 'Trucial chiefs' of 'the Pirate coast' are bound by treaty engagements, many of which date back to 1820, to grant neither political nor commercial concessions to a third party without the consent of the British Government, in return for which they are guaranteed in their own territorial and political independence, while they are held responsible for observing and maintaining the peace of the Gulf. Great Britain, in short, polices the waters and shores, both as a strategical necessity and because British commercial interests, particularly of the Indian empire, are vitally concerned in the routes and traffic of this great arm of the Indian Ocean.

In the last fifteen years the carefully planned scheme of the Bagdad railway has brought the Euphrates valley, Persia, and the Persian Gulf into the centre of European politics. The chief feature of the scheme is the proposal to graft on to the Anatolian railway (under German control) from Scutari to Konia a transcontinental line crossing the Taurus range at Adana, thence *via* Mosul and Bagdad to Basra, and continuing thence to Koweit or a port further east at the head of the Gulf, thus connecting the Mediterranean with the Indian Ocean by an inland route, which at its western end through Constantinople can be made continuous with the railways running to Ostend or Hamburg, and at its eastern terminus could be extended through southern Persia and Baluchistan to Karachi and Bombay. In the complicated controversies which the proposal involved, two points alone can be mentioned here : (1) With whom was the political control to rest ? A decadent and impoverished Turkish empire could only construct the line by full 'concessions' in return for the foreign capital invested. As the line from Konia to Basra must run wholly through Turkish territory, it was clear that the nation which found the money would control not only the line but the Turkish empire through which it passed, and the German company that had obtained the concessions could and would probably become a mere agency of the German Government, whose political influence in Turkey was already formidable and organized. (2) If the line stopped short at Basra, its *raison d'être* was seriously impaired ; but as soon as it ended in a terminus on the Persian Gulf a grave military menace arose for British India, for Koweit was within striking distance of the British frontier, apart from the imperilling of British political interests in the Gulf itself. And Great Britain was in a position to insist on adequate guarantees before permitting the section from Basra to Kuweit (which is not in Turkish territory) to be authorized or constructed. Russian interest through her Caucasian and Trans-Caspian territories and in northern Persia was not less than that of Great Britain, though it applied to a different section of the line. The history of the railway and the conventions which its construction have brought about will be found detailed in a Parliamentary Paper (Cd. 5635) of 1911. Economic equality on the route and a definite settlement of the position in the Persian Gulf were the conditions laid down by Great Britain as essential to the strategic and commercial interests of British India ; and in 1914 the negotiations over the section from Basra to Kuweit had not resulted in a final settlement. Nevertheless the construction of the line was proceeding steadily. From Konia to Basra the distance on the projected scheme is about 1,400 miles, and of these about 550 had already been laid down, leaving about 850 still to be constructed. In its broadest aspect the Bagdad railway is the most ambitious of many projects for the reorganization and rejuvenation of the Turkish empire in Asia which are bound up with the future of the Turkish empire as a whole. That future, as already pointed out, centres as much round Constantinople as round Anatolia and the Euphrates valley. The Bagdad railway from Scutari to Basra as planned rests on the assumption that Constantinople is and remains Turkish, and that the numerous 'feeders' to the trunk line will link it up with Turkish ports on the coasts of Asia Minor and Syria. Hence, until the future of the Ottoman empire both in Asia and in Europe has been definitely settled, and its international relations and position finally cleared up, the railway will remain, as in the past, an incomplete and mutilated project. But once that future has been settled the railway will simply be a problem for engineers and for financiers—a question of routes and of money ; and when completed, a new chapter in the economic development of Anatolia and the rich Euphrates valley will begin. That it will supersede the water route *via* the Suez Canal seems very doubtful. Its justification lies in the commercial possibilities that it will open up for the areas that it traverses.

Plate XXXIV. A comparison of the map of Africa in 1800 with that in 1914 is highly instructive, for the difference between the two contains both the history of extended and patient geographical discovery and exploration, and the elaborate process compressed mainly into the period from 1880 to 1914, by which the vast continent has been parcelled out between the European states expanding beyond European waters. The northern coast of Africa from Morocco to the peninsula of Sinai and Syria, where it joins the continent of Asia, geographically belongs to the Mediterranean area and system, cut off by the girdle of mountains and the deserts of their hinterland from the rest of the vast continent of which it is a part. The history of this portion is primarily European, secondarily Asiatic, and only in the last degree African. The political control or occupation of Morocco, Algeria, Tunisia, Tripoli, and Egypt has been the history of the advance and regression of the Mohammedan conquerors of the seventh to the fifteenth centuries, whose territories by the sixteenth century formed part of the Ottoman empire—and the political distribution registered in the map of 1914 sums up the gradual dismemberment of that Ottoman empire and its subject-provinces and feudatories. For the rest of Africa a map of 1800 represents a fringe of European settlements and trading stations : French, Dutch, and British at Senegal and on the Gold Coast, Portuguese from Calabar to Cape Negro, Dutch and British at the Cape of Good Hope and in Natal, Portuguese along the Mozambique Channel and from Cape Delgado to the Straits of Bab-el-Mandeb, unoccupied by any European power even on the coast fringes, while the remaining nine-tenths of the interior form a vast area, unknown, unexplored, and represented by a significant blank or dotted with hypothetical names. Until the explorers and a century of commercial penetration had done their work, the political distribution or occupation was bound to wait on the achievements of the traveller and geographer. When the course and character of the four great rivers—the Nile, the Niger, the Congo, and the Zambesi—had been ascertained with comparative accuracy, Africa was ripe for distribution under the competitive pressure of an expanding Europe, the major states of which were seeking for areas of commercial importance or for strategical positions to strengthen dominions or territories acquired elsewhere. British advance in Africa, for example, has been a combination of three powerful motor-forces—trade, dating back to the slave trade from the Guinea coast of the seventeenth century, the need of strategical points to control (e. g. Cape Town) the uninterrupted sea route to India, and territories which could be made true colonies, i. e. where white men and women could live, breed, and die. It is noticeable above all that the map of 1914 is the expression of elaborate international arrangements, conventions, and delimiting boundary commissions, with the result that all of Africa (with the exception of Abyssinia, Liberia, and Morocco) has now been allotted, and further advance by any European state is only possible by exchange or by the compulsory acquisition of territory from a European rival and neighbour. It is only possible here to indicate the chief features of this vast partition, the evolution and details of which can be traced in J. S. Keltie's *The Partition of Africa* and H. H. Johnston's *History of the Colonization of Africa*. The critical date in the modern epoch was 1884, when Germany entered as a serious competitor into the acquisition of African territory by proclaiming a protectorate over Damaraland and Namaqualand and annexing Togoland and the Cameroons. In the same year the Berlin Conference recognized the Congo State, which had been founded by Leopold II of Belgium—and which in 1908 was transferred to the Belgian kingdom. Since 1884 the process of partition has proceeded with remarkable rapidity. A series of European agreements between 1886 and 1906 practically defined the lines as now drawn, with certain exceptions noted below. No less than seven European states are represented, viz. Great Britain, France, Germany, Portugal, Spain, Italy, and Belgium. Spain and Italy have the smallest shares, though Italy has recently added to her territories in Somaliland and Eritrea the Turkish province of Tripoli (1912). But only Great Britain and Germany have their possessions so divided as to give them a direct interest in every part of Africa, and Germany is excluded from the Mediterranean area. Reckoned in mere superficial extent of territory, France is the largest of African proprietors, ruling over some 3,700,000 square miles, as compared with the 3,300,000 of British territory (including Egypt) and the 930,000 square miles of German. The French African empire, it is also noticeable, is confined to a vast block in the west and west central districts, and unless the island of Madagascar be deemed to be African, France has no foothold in the south and east of the continent, with the trifling exception of French Somaliland. The British possessions, however, have three distinctive features : (a) They are grouped on the shores of each of the waters that wash the continent—the Mediterranean, the Red Sea, the Indian Ocean, and the Atlantic, and at four critical points, aided by possessions outside Africa proper, they control strategic lines of the first importance. Gibraltar, Aden and Socotra, Zanzibar, St. Helena, and Cape Town have and confer a military and naval significance indisputable and incomparable. (b) In the solid block of British South Africa Great Britain possesses the one great area fitted to be a colony for the white races. German South-West Africa competes, it is true, with this, but under demonstrably unfavourable conditions, and the Union of South Africa, which has achieved the unity of the British and Dutch races under the British flag, and which is one of the great self-governing Dominions in the empire, is an African state with a tradition, a character, an organization, and a future that make it unique in the political divisions of Africa. (c) Of the four great African rivers—the Nile, the Niger, the Zambesi, and the Congo—British territory controls or shares in the control of the three first. Mastery of the arterial rivers of a huge continent, as the history of the American continent proves, is a brief expression of the great truth that political power follows and rests on the trunk waterways. What the Danube, the Rhine, and the Vistula have been to the Europe of the past, the Nile, the Zambesi, the Niger, and the Congo will be to the Africa of the future. For a great river can be the perpetual cradle of a great civilization.

Egypt and Morocco occupy a peculiar and distinctive position amongst the African states. In 1780 Egypt was nominally a pashalik of the Ottoman empire, though real power in the country was exercised by the Beys, who formed a military oligarchy. Napoleon, in 1798, made a great effort to conquer the province for France, which was defeated by Nelson's victory in the Bay of Aboukir and by the expulsion of the French, thanks to an Anglo-Indian force, in 1801. Egypt then was restored to Turkish rule, and from 1811 to 1849 its history is bound up with the extraordinary career, abilities, and ambitions of the Albanian chief, Mehemet Ali, who made himself master of the country, twice at least made war on the Porte, and finally, in 1841, was granted for himself and his heirs the 'pashalik' as an hereditary possession, subject to an annual tribute to the Sultan at Constantinople. His descendant Ismail, by Firmans granted in 1866 and 1872, secured the confirmation and extension of these privileges, together with the title of Khedive, which made him practically the independent ruler of a separate state—Turkish suzerainty being pared down to a minimum of theoretical overlordship. Ismail's extravagance in 1876 brought about international financial intervention—'the Dual Control', by which an English and a French official supervised the financial administration, and in 1879 Ismail was deposed. The rebellion of Arabi led, in 1882, to a British military occupation which restored the Khedivial Government and which has lasted ever since. The diplomatic position was further complicated by the Anglo-Egyptian reconquest of the Sudan (lost in 1884), between 1892 and 1898, in the reoccupation and organization of which Great Britain claimed and maintained a joint authority with the Egyptian Government, and by the international status of the Suez Canal, completed and opened in 1869, and the position of which was defined by the Convention of 1888, subsequently modified by the Anglo-French Convention of 1904. This important agreement, preceding by three years the Convention with Russia, brought to an end the dispute which had seriously embittered the relations between Great Britain and France since 1882. France, in return for concessions in Morocco, practically recognized the permanent British occupation of Egypt and agreed to consider in the most friendly manner proposals which it had hitherto obstructed or opposed for reforms in the government and administration of the country. In plain words, France recognized the *de facto* British protectorate. The formal declaration of that protectorate, the severance of the nominal dependence of Egypt on the Turkish Sultan, and the elevation of a new Khedive to the rank and title of Sultan (December 19, 1914) were the logical conclusion, under the pressure of exceptional circumstances, of the Convention of 1904, and were promptly recognized as such by the French Government. Egypt can now, therefore, be definitely placed in the category of protectorates under the British empire—what it had virtually been since 1892 or 1882.

Morocco—the shereefian empire, consisting of the kingdoms of Fez and Morocco—is the westernmost of the Barbary states, and the only one which has survived into the twentieth century. The inland frontier, save where it adjoins the Spanish Rio de Oro, marches with the frontiers of French Algeria and West Africa, and France therefore has a greater interest in the internal prosperity and order of Morocco than any other state, while the control of the ports, at Tangier, Mogador, and Casablanca, by a foreign rival would be a menace both to Spain, France, and Great Britain (at Gibraltar). After twice (in 1905 and 1911) being nearly the cause of a European war, in consequence of German efforts to secure a footing in the country, the status of Morocco now rests on three international conventions—the Anglo-French of April 8, 1904, the Algeciras Convention of April 7, 1906, and the Franco-German agreement of February 1909—by which the finances, trade, customs, and administrative machinery were reorganized and the right of France to maintain order was defined. The Rif country, with the exception of Tangier, was recognized as a Spanish sphere, and fortifications that would impair the position of Gibraltar were prohibited. Finally, by the Franco-Moroccan Treaty of March 1912, a French protectorate was proclaimed, preserving the treaty rights of all foreign powers and maintaining the political status of the Sultan, under French control. Germany in 1913 gave its assent to this treaty. In return for German acquiescence in these arrangements, a strip of the French Congo adjoining the German Cameroons was ceded to Germany, and the new frontier was delimited in 1908. Morocco has therefore become for France what Egypt has become for Great Britain : a protectorate in which the freedom of action of the protecting power has been recognized by the government or governments hitherto most opposed to it. Morocco indeed points the plain moral—that between 'commercial penetration' and political control there is no satisfactory half-way stage, and indirect political control by an irresponsible financial or commercial syndicate or company is far more dangerous and harmful than the direct political control of a state, responsible for its actions, whose contracts can be made a part of the public law, in the maintenance of which all civilized communities have an equal interest. The sanctions of international law may be still very weak and unsatisfactory, but the history of Africa since 1880 proves that the most obstinate of disputes can be solved by international agreement, and that insistence on the binding force of public engagements creates the public conscience which recognizes that minorities no less than majorities have rights, and that economic claims imply political and social duties in the governments that would enforce them. The perfectibility of mankind may be an academic superstition or a philosophic chimera, but experience has shown that as a working hypothesis of government, particularly in the relations of the white to subject races, it can achieve remarkable results both for the governors and the governed.

Plates XXXV and XXXVI introduce the problems of the Pacific and the unsolved future of the Chinese empire. The map of the Far East records the early history of the entry of European states, the modern development displacing some of the earliest of the competitors, the belated entry of Germany on the scene, and the emergence of Japan from mediaeval paralysis and isolation to a position of first rank in the Eastern powers. Of the three earliest of European colonizing states—Spain, Portugal, and the Dutch—the Dutch alone have retained a substantial foothold in their rich and important possessions of Java, Sumatra, the Celebes Islands, Timor, and New Guinea. The Portuguese, who led the way alike to East Africa, the Indian peninsula, the Persian Gulf, and the Chinese seas, are represented only by Macao and one-half of the island of Timor. Spain has practically disappeared. In 1898 she ceded the Philippine Islands to the United States, and in 1899 sold the Marianne, Caroline, and Pelew group to Germany. Great Britain and France have steadily added to their possessions. The acquisition of Assam (1826), Pegu (1852), and Upper Burma (1886) brought the British frontier on the mainland up to the Chinese. The Straits Settlements with Singapore (1819), Hong Kong (1841, extended in 1860 and 1898), Labuan (1846), the Malay States (1874), North Borneo (by 1881), part of New Guinea (1884), Sarawak and Brunei (1888), and Wei-hai-wei in 1898, complete the list. Meanwhile the French had built up in Indo-China an eastern province only second in importance to their African empire. Saigon (1859), Cambodia (1863), Tonkin (1865), western Cochin-China (1867), Annam (1884), mark the main stages of acquisition, while their advance to the Me Kong river (1893) threatened the absorption or dismemberment of Siam, which was, however, averted by the Anglo-French agreement of 1896. Anticipating the lines of the Anglo-Russian Persian Convention of 1907, Siam was divided into an eastern or French sphere, a western or British sphere, and a central or neutral and independent sphere. And as a consequence Great Britain assumed a protectorate over the Malay States not already directly annexed. Russia had steadily expanded southwards from Kamchatka. By 1875 she had brought her frontiers down to Korea, held the Amur river and Saghalin Islands, and was established at Vladivostok. Manchuria and Korea, the mastery of the Bay of Pechili, and the possession of a southern and warm-water port at Port Arthur (to be the terminus of the magnificent transcontinental railway connecting the Far Eastern seas across

Siberia with Moscow and Petrograd) seemed to be the natural consequence of this irresistible advance and absorption. The opposition came not from European Powers, as elsewhere, but from an Eastern monarchy. Japan had with unparalleled rapidity and success, in the forty years from 1859, transformed herself from an Oriental feudalism to a Europeanized state, and the war with China in 1894 revealed her ambition to compete on equal terms with the greatest of European states. Forced in 1895 by the triple combination of France, Russia, and Germany to give back the Liao-Tung Peninsula to China, though she retained Formosa and the Pescadores Islands, and to see Russia acquire Port Arthur (1898) and Manchuria (1900), she challenged her most dangerous rival in 1904, and the Treaty of Portsmouth, of 1905, which ended the Russo-Japanese War, drove Russia out of Manchuria (restored to China), put Port Arthur and the Liao-Tung Peninsula in Japanese possession, together with the control of Korea (annexed in 1910) and the southern half of Saghalin. Japan had thus secured a large territory on the mainland and completely vindicated her claim to equality in Far Eastern affairs with the European Powers. The Anglo-Japanese Treaty of alliance of 1905 (renewed and revised in 1911) set the seal on these achievements, and it has led to a final settlement with Russia in the agreement of 1911, which guaranteed the maintenance of the existing *status quo*, and removed all the outstanding causes of dispute.

The political and economic problems of the Far East and of the Pacific are so numerous and so complex as to make speculation, however fascinating, as uncertain as prophecy. Four factors, however, can be specified which are certain to exercise a dominant influence : (1) The action of Germany in compelling the cession of Kiao-Chau (1898) and the establishment of a strongly fortified naval and commercial base on Chinese territory, followed as it was by the Russian acquisition of Port Arthur and the British occupation of Wei-hai-wei, brought the territorial future of China at once into the forefront. Vast as China is, she is no sphere for European colonies, but her teeming and intelligent population, enormous and compact territories and undeveloped resources, make her an unlimited field for railways, commercial penetration, and concessions. What the value of the numerous international agreements from 1899 to 1914, laying down the independence and integrity of China and defining vague spheres of international action, may be, the future alone can show. The downfall of the Manchu dynasty after two and a half centuries of rule, and the establishment of a Republic (recognized by the European Powers) in 1912, are not the least astonishing of the recent events in the Far East. And at the gates of China stands Japan, whose plans and dreams ' have hands and feet '. In Africa and central Asia expanding or aggressive European states have found their chief difficulties in the jealousies and opposition of European rivals. But in the Far East the unique position, power, and ambitions of Japan have enabled an Oriental empire to challenge and defeat European advance, and if a republican China can repeat the achievements of Japan it would be folly to prophesy about the future. (2) The irresistible outflow of the superabundant populations of China and Japan on to the North and South American coasts, into the Pacific Islands, and to the continent of Australia, is a feature which the future will accentuate, not diminish. A ' white America ' and a ' white Australia ' proclaim ideals which will not be achieved without a prolonged effort that will tax all the resources of statesmanship and raise all the problems of race, colour, religion, and social ethics and standards, the full import of which the European races have as yet scarcely realized. And behind the problems of race, colour, religion, and conflicting civilizations at very different stages of development are working vast economic motor-forces on a scale and in a theatre unparalleled in the cramped world of Europe. (3) The completion of the Panama Canal brings the eastern half of the Pacific into direct connexion, under American control, with the Atlantic and with Europe. Above all, it establishes the United States as a Pacific Power in a wholly new framework and outlook—and one peculiar to herself. The establishment of the United States at Samoa and in the Philippines speaks for itself. (4) The problems of the Pacific are essentially British problems. The United States of North America, the Latin states of South America, Russia, France, Germany, China, and Japan, are all obviously Pacific Powers, but Great Britain is the only Power with the strategic and territorial position which gives her a direct interest in all parts of the Pacific at one and the same time. Plate XXXV has to be supplemented by Plate XXXVI to bring out the full significance of this conclusion. From Wei-hai-wei to Hong Kong and Singapore, from Borneo through New Guinea to Australia and New Zealand and the Fiji Islands, the eye catches the Falkland Islands lying across the route round Cape Horn, before it travels northwards to the solid mass of the Dominion of Canada—a strategic ring united by the unifying seas, but more significant by reason of the character of its component links. It is the self-governing Commonwealth of Australia and the Dominions of New Zealand and Canada, at once separate states conscious of an individual state life and organic members of a greater imperial whole, which differentiate the British empire in the Pacific specifically from other European Powers. They have stations, but Great Britain

alone is represented by states as well as by stations. It is a difference akin to that which, as has already been pointed out, distinguishes the Union of South Africa from the colonial dependencies of the European Powers in the African continent. The policy of Russia, France, Germany, or Holland in the Pacific will be decided at Petrograd, Paris, Berlin, or Amsterdam by the Dutch, German, French, and Russian nations in Europe, and the policy of Great Britain also would be decided in London if her possessions were limited to her stations in the Far East. But to-day, and increasingly so in the future, behind the decisions of British policy will lie the will of Australia, New Zealand, and Canada, and a growing Canadian and Australasian executive strength to mould and enforce those decisions. Japan and the United States have already attained maturity. Behind them to-day are the forces of maturity. Hence their strength and their claims. But Canada, New Zealand, and Australia stand on the threshold of the dawn. A Canada and a greater Australasia that look to populations of scores of millions of inhabitants, English speaking and sharing in and contributing to the unity of the heritage of a common British civilization, no less firmly planted in South Africa than in the grey and misty waters of the North Sea, can face the future of the Pacific, no matter what that future may have in store, without fear or misgiving. They stand for the British empire, and the British empire stands behind them.

STATISTICS

AUSTRIA-HUNGARY.

(See Int. pp. 13-15. Plates XVIII-XXI)

The following Austro-Hungarian statistics are official, but are not absolutely trustworthy. Those for Hungary in particular are suspected by good authorities of having been manipulated for political purposes.

AUSTRIA

Population by census of 1910. 28,571,934	Estimated population in 1910. 28,995,844

Divided on basis of language :

German	9,950,266	Serbs and Croats	783,334
Czech and Slovak	6,435,983	Italian and Latin	768,422
Poles	4,967,984	Roumanian	275,115
Ruthenes	3,518,854	Magyar	10,974
Slovenes	1,252,940		

HUNGARY

Population 1900. 19,254,559	Population 1910. 20,886,487	
	1900.	1910.
Magyar	8,742,301	10,050,575
German	2,135,181	2,037,435
Slovak	2,079,641	1,967,970
Roumanian	2,799,479	2,949,032
Ruthenes	429,447	472,587
Croats	1,682,104	1,833,162
Serbs	1,048,645	1,106,471
Others	397,791	469,255

GERMAN AND RUSSIAN POLAND

(Int. pp. 17-18. Plates XXVII, XXVIII, and XXIX)

In the German census of 1900 the figures given are :

Poles (speaking German and Polish)	.	169,654
„ („ only Polish)	.	3,086,489

About 85 per cent. belong to the provinces of Posen and West and East Prussia ; in 1905, 61.21 per cent. of the province of Posen were Poles.

In the last Russian census (1897) the population of Russian Poland was given as 9,388,801, of which Poles numbered 7,394,712, Jews 1,267,194.

The Central Statistical Committee estimated the population of Russian Poland for 1912 at 12,776,100, of which 10,740,000 are estimated to be Poles.

The total Polish population of the historic kingdom of Poland (Plates XXVIII and XXIX)—excluding Lithuania—may thus be broadly estimated to-day at not less than :

Russian Poles	.	.	10,740,000
Prussian Poles	.	.	3,300,000
Austro-Hungarian Poles	.	5,000,000
			19,040,000

FINLAND

(P. 19 and Plates XXX and XXXI)

The census of 1901 gave a total population of 2,713,000, of which were :

Finns	.	.	.	2,353,000
Swedes	.	.	.	350,000
Others	.	.	.	10,000

TURKEY IN ASIA

(Pp. 16-17. Plate XXVI)

No figures can be relied on. The following estimates are taken from *The Statesman's Year Book* (1915 ed.) for what they are worth :

	Mussulmans.	Armenians.	Other Christians.	Jews.
Asia Minor	7,179,900	576,200	972,300	184,600
Armenia	1,795,800	480,700	165,200	30,700
Aleppo	192,500	49,000	134,300	29,000
Beyrût	230,200	6,100	160,400	138,800
Lebanon	30,400	—	319,300	49,800
Aegean Islands	27,200	—	296,800	—
	9,456,000	1,112,000	2,048,300	432,600

Making a total estimated population of 13,038,300.

THE BALKAN STATES

(Pp. 13-16. Plates XVIII and XXII-XXV)

The populations of the Balkan States before the First and Second Balkan Wars (1912-3) were estimated to be :

		Population.	Area in sq. miles.
Roumania	.	7,230,418	50,720
Bulgaria .	.	4,337,516	33,647
Serbia .	.	2,911,701	18,650
Montenegro	.	250,000	3,474
Greece .	.	2,666,000	25,014
Turkey in Europe	.	6,130,200	65,350

By the Treaty of Bucharest (July 26, O.S., 1913)—

		Population.	Area : sq. miles.
* Roumania *gained*		286,000	*gained* 2,687
Bulgaria	,,	125,490	,, 9,663
Serbia	,,	1,636,291	,, 15,241
Montenegro	,,	230,000	,, 2,129
Greece	,,	1,697,000	,, 16,919
Turkey in Europe *lost*		4,239,200	*lost* 54,468

* The acquisitions of Bulgaria, Serbia, Montenegro, and Greece were at the expense of Turkey ; but the Roumanian acquisition was at the expense of Bulgaria, which ceded territory previously Bulgarian.

The Roumanians outside Roumania are estimated at :

In Hungary	.	.	,	.	2,949,032
,, Bessarabia (Russian)	.	.		.	1,100,000
					4,049,032

ITALY

(P. 12. Plates XVI-XVIII)

The Italians in the Trentino are estimated at	.	560,000
,, ,, ,, Trieste and Istria ,, ,,	.	180,000
		740,000

SWITZERLAND

(Pp. 11, 12. Plate XV)

The census of 1911 gives the population at			3,781,430
of which there were German speaking	.	.	2,599,154
French ,,	.	.	796,244
Italian ,,	.	.	301,325
Roumansch ,,	.	.	39,834

ALSACE-LORRAINE

(Pp. 9, 11. Plate IX)

The Reichsland of Elsass-Lothringen (Alsace-Lorraine), annexed to the German empire in 1871, had an area of 5,604 square miles and a population (in 1910) of 1,874,014 inhabitants.

Erratum

The explanatory note in Plate XXV—Balkan States in 1914— should read as follows (and not as printed on the map) :

Greek Frontier as settled in 1881.

Territory ceded by Greece to Turkey in 1897.

Frontier of Greece as settled *after the Greek War of Independence by the Treaty of London, 1830.*

Acquisitions of Bulgaria *between 1886 and 1913.*

EUROPE—DENSITY OF POPULATION

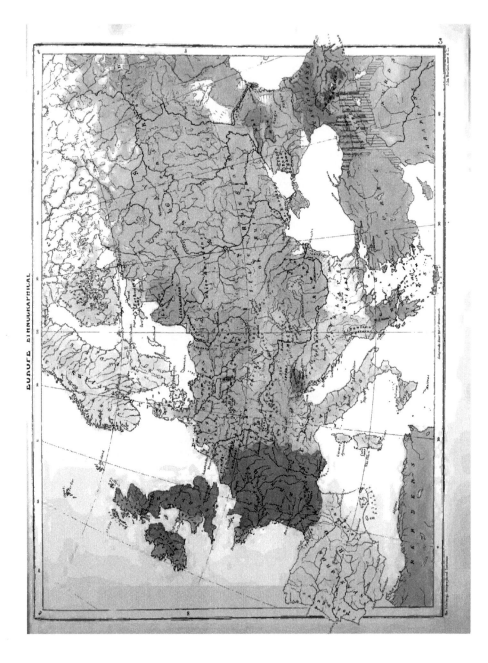

CENTRAL EUROPE—INDUSTRIAL

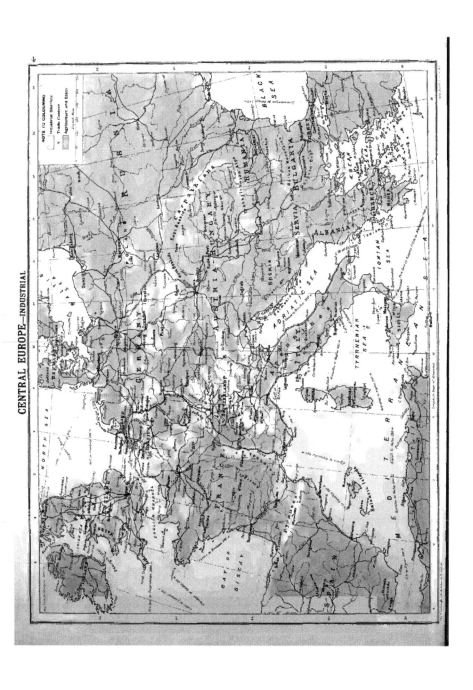

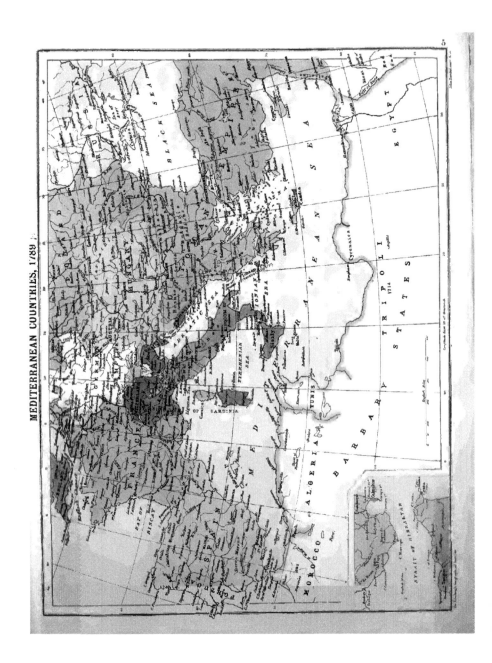

MEDITERRANEAN COUNTRIES, 1789.

MEDITERRANEAN COUNTRIES, 1914

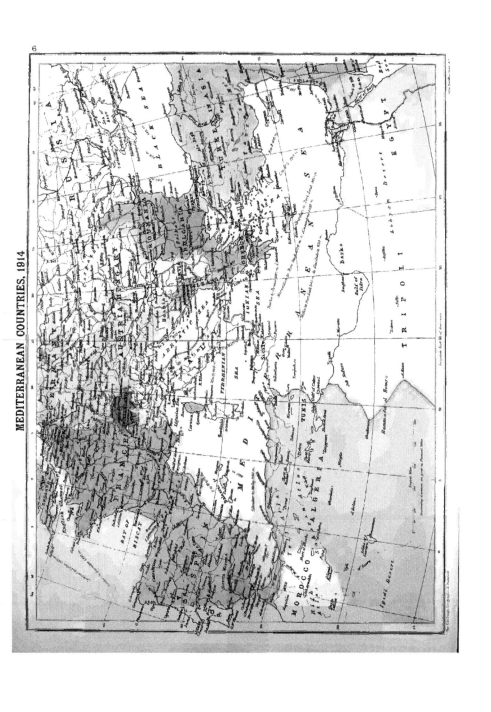

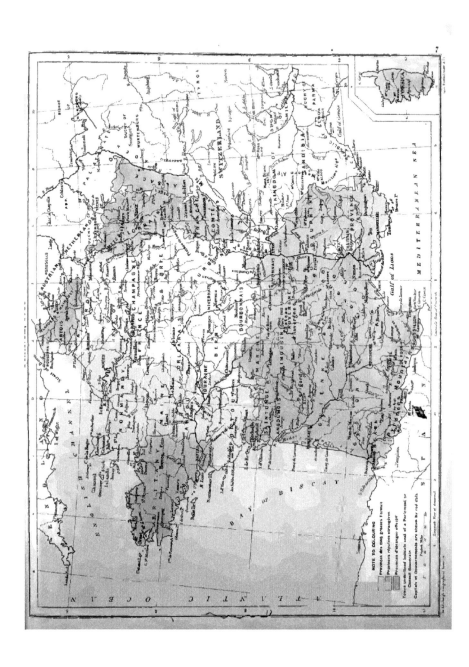

FRENCH EMPIRE, 1810

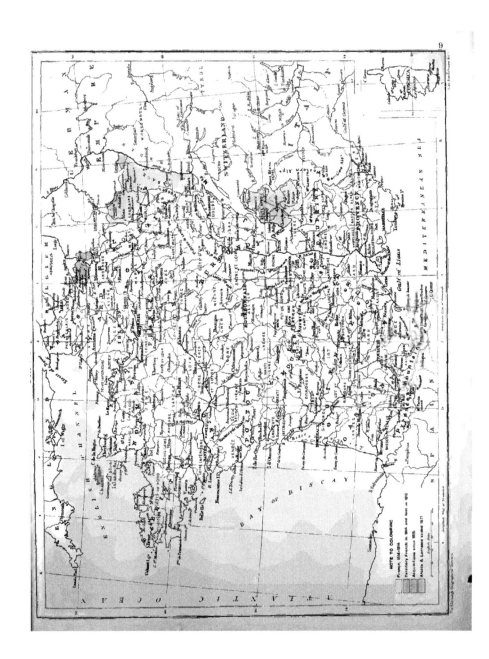

HOLLAND AND BELGIUM

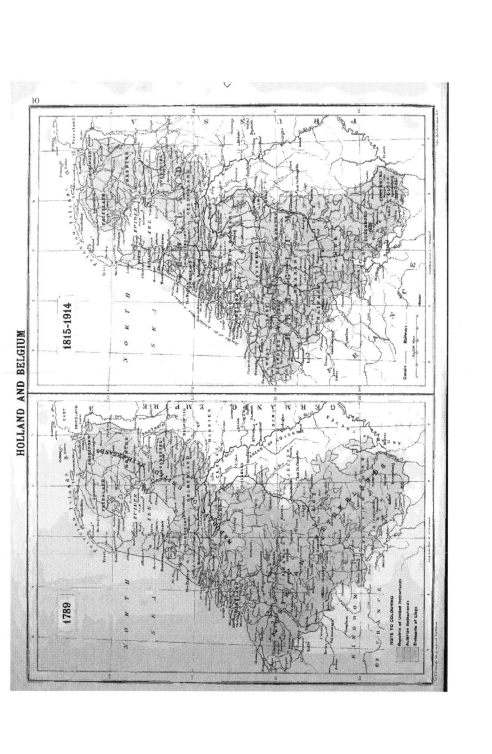

1815-1914

1789

NOTE TO COLORING
Republic of United Netherlands
Austrian Netherlands
Bishopric of Liege

Canals   Railways

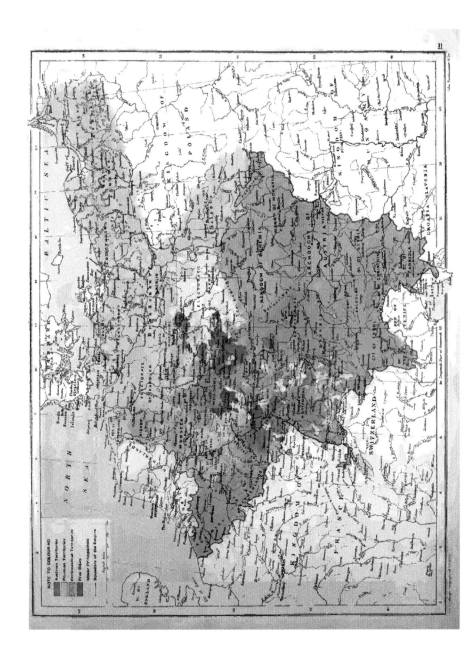

GERMANY, 1810

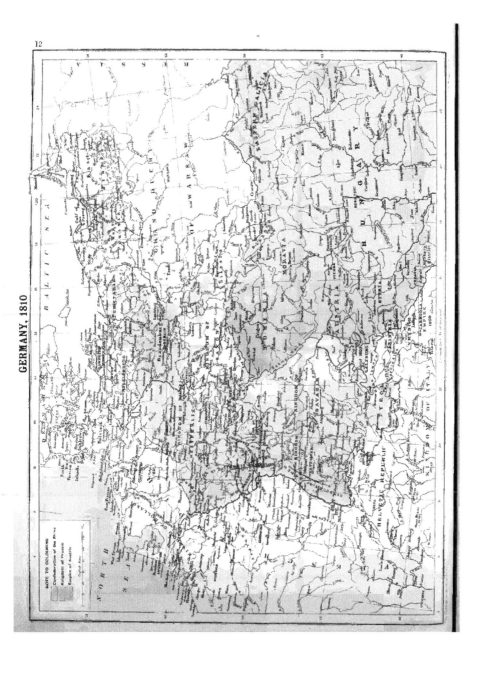

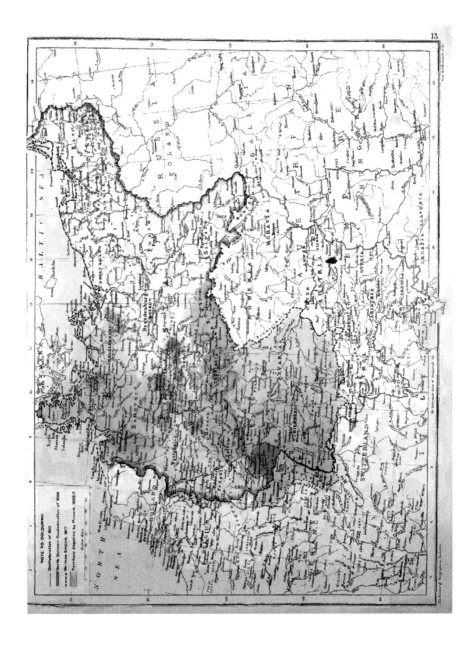

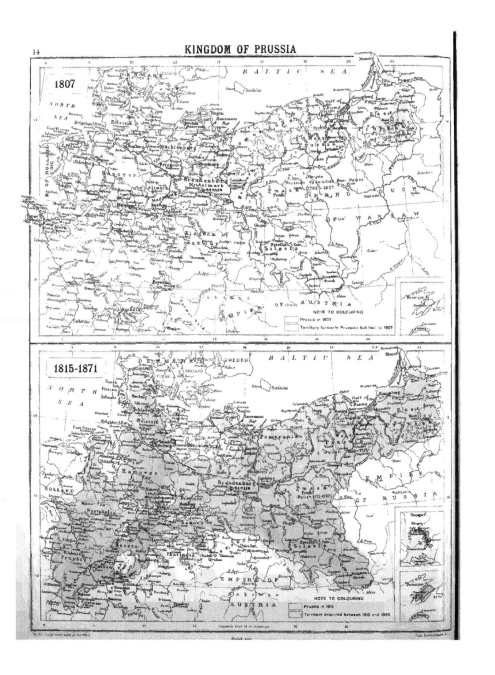

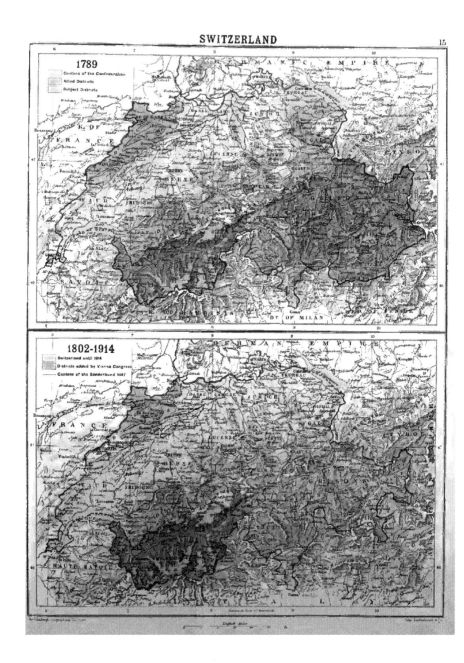

1789

Cantons of the Confederation
Allied Districts
Subject Districts

1802-1914

Switzerland until 1914
Districts added by Vienna Congress
Cantons of the Sonderbund 1847

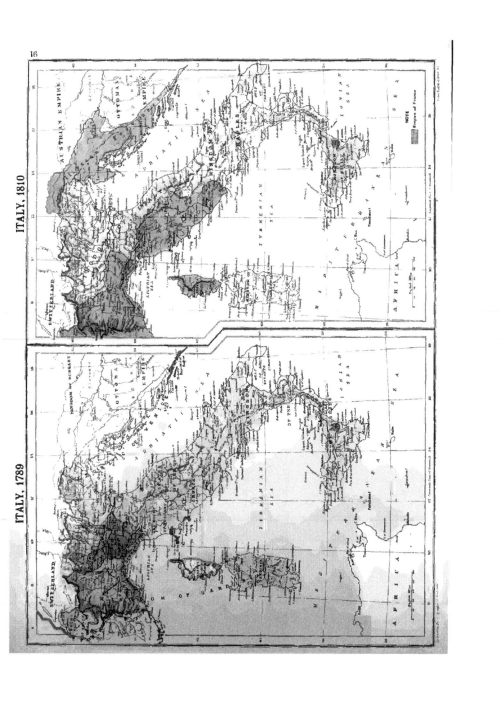

ITALY, 1810

ITALY, 1789

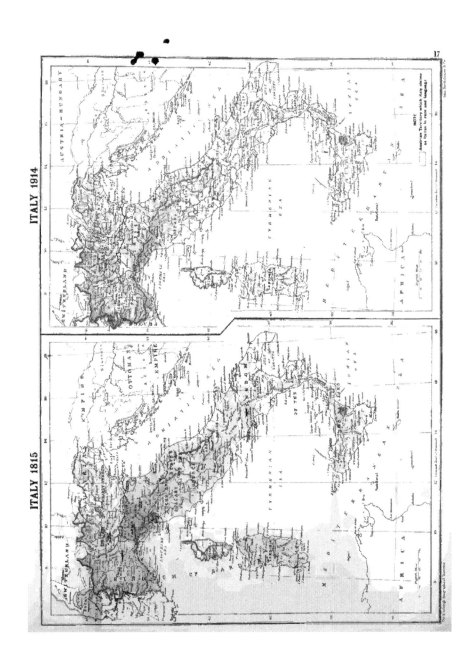

ITALY 1914

ITALY 1815

John Bartholomew &Co

AUSTRIA-HUNGARY & BALKAN STATES—ETHNOGRAPHICAL

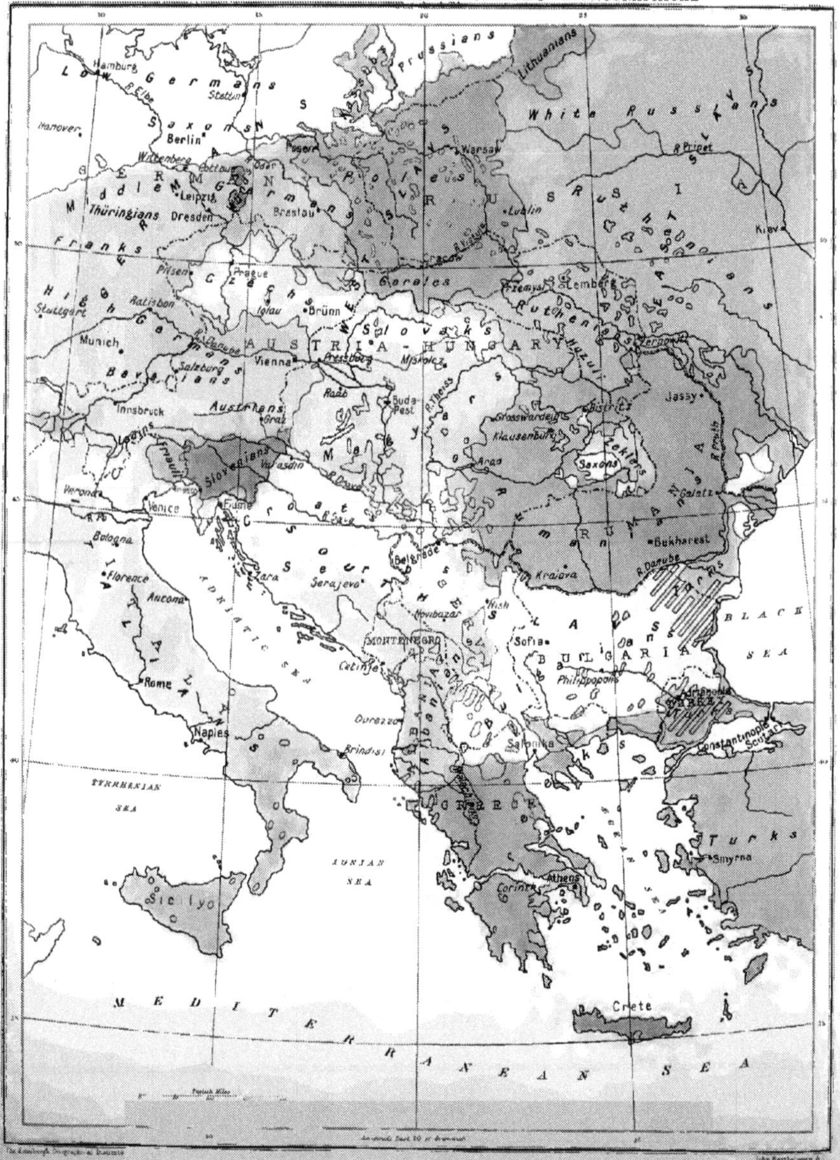

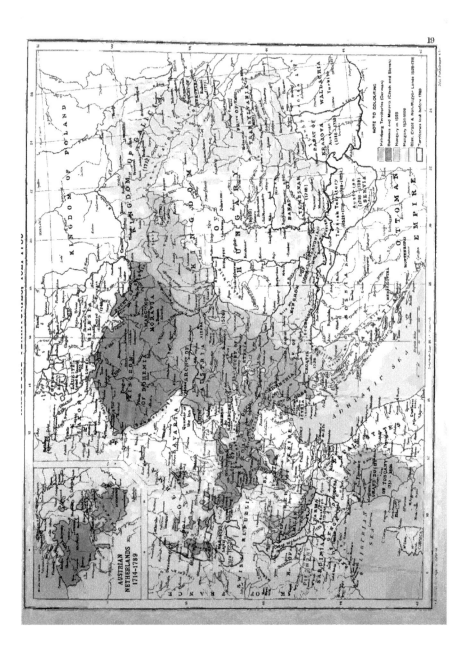

AUSTRIAN
NETHERLANDS
1714-1789

NOTE TO COLOURING

Salzburg Territories (Germany)

Bohemia and Moravia (Czech and Slovak)

Hungary in 1520

Hungary 1526-1699

Slav, Croat & Non-Magyar Lands 1526-1780

Territories lost before 1780

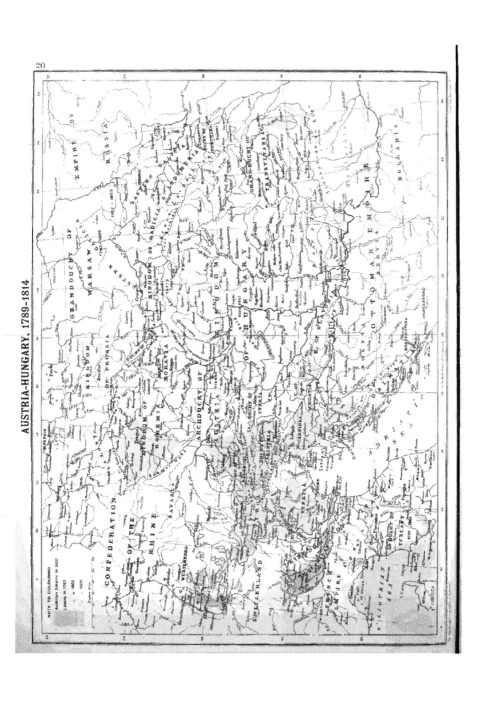

AUSTRIA-HUNGARY, 1789-1814

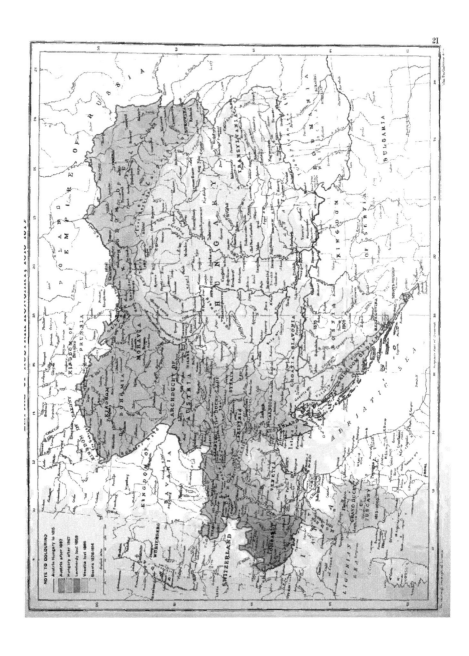

NOTE TO COLOURING
Ottoman Empire 1789
Servian Kingdom under Stephen Dushan c. 1350
Bulgarian Kingdom of Simeon in 927

HUNGARY

TRANSYLVANIA

BUCOWINA
Lost to Austria
1777

LITTLE TARTARY

MOLDAVIA

VIENNA

BUDA PEST

BANAT OF TEMESVAR
Lost by Turkey
1718

BANAT OF KRAJOVA
1718 - 1739

WALLACHIA

BUCAREST

BOSNIA

SERVIA

BULGARIA

BLACK SEA

HERZEGOVINA

MONTENEGRO

ADRIATIC SEA

CONSTANTINOPLE

SEA OF MARMORA

EPIRUS

THESSALY

IONIAN SEA

ARCHIPELAGO

CYCLADES

ARGOLIS

CANDIA OR CRETE

English Miles

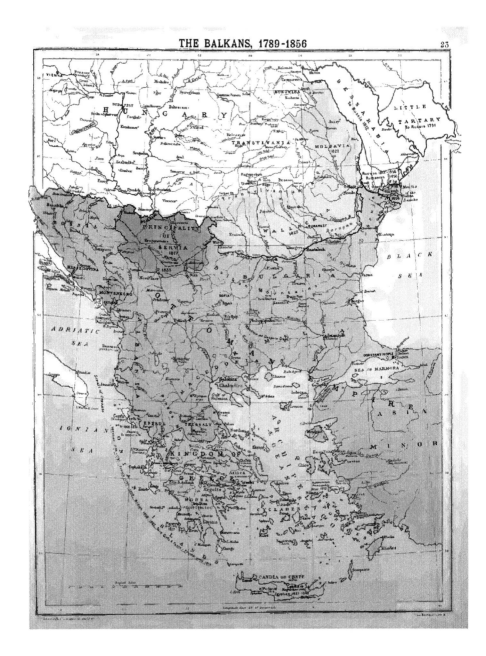

THE BALKANS, 1856-1878

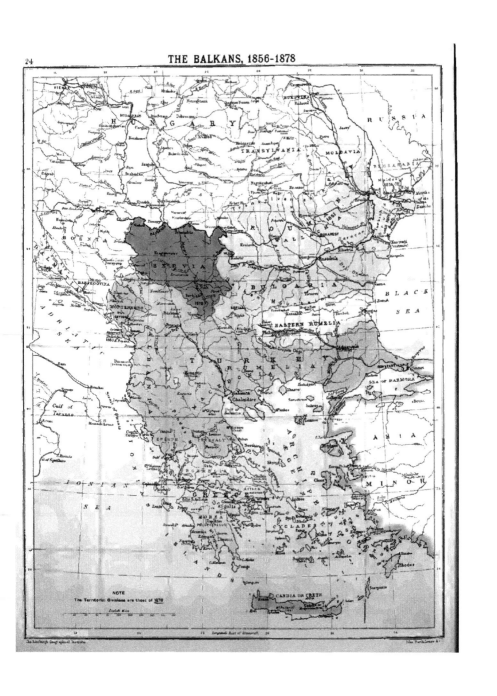

NOTE
The Territorial Divisions are those of 1878

English Miles

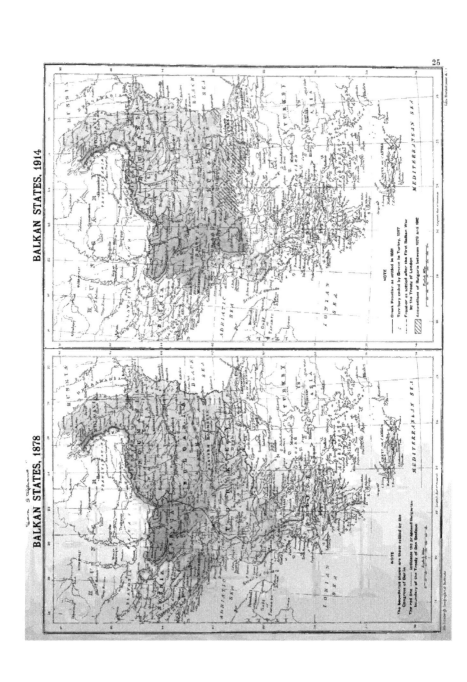

BALKAN STATES, 1914

BALKAN STATES, 1878

THE OTTOMAN EMPIRE IN ASIA, 1815-1914

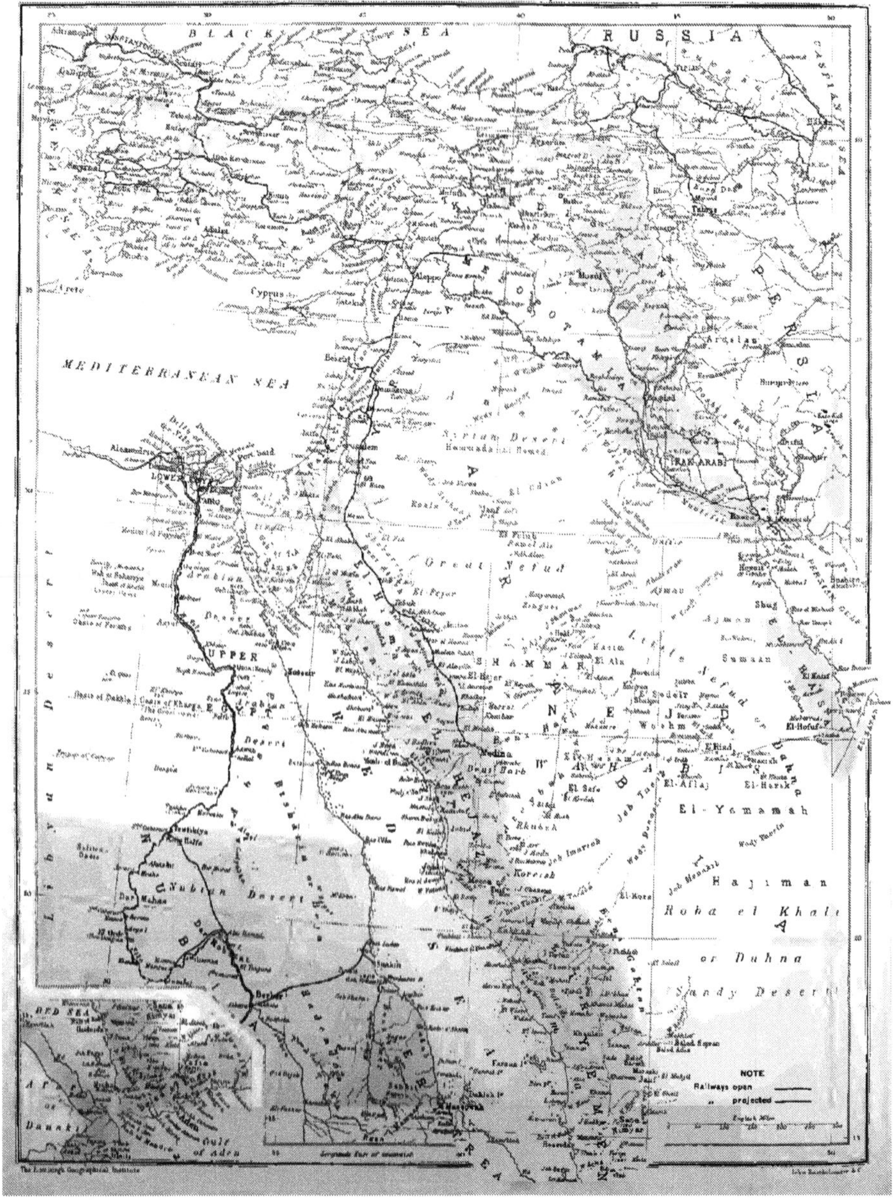

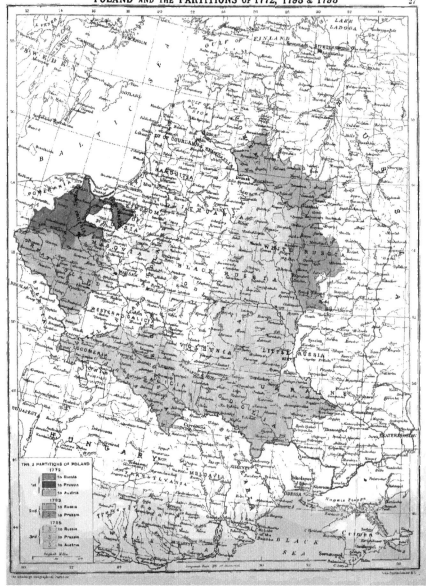

THE 3 PARTITIONS OF POLAND

1772
1st
- to Russia
- to Prussia
- to Austria

1793
2nd
- to Russia
- to Prussia

1795
3rd
- to Russia
- to Prussia
- to Austria

NOTE TO COLOURING

Poland as constituted in 1815
Poland before partition of 1772

English Miles

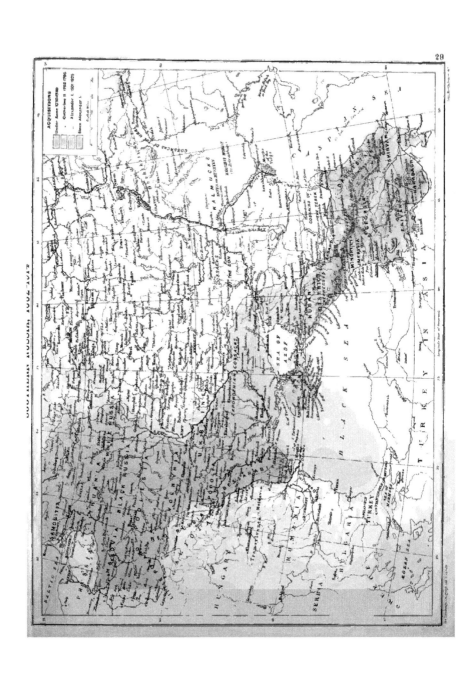

SOUTHERN RUSSIA, 1801–1917

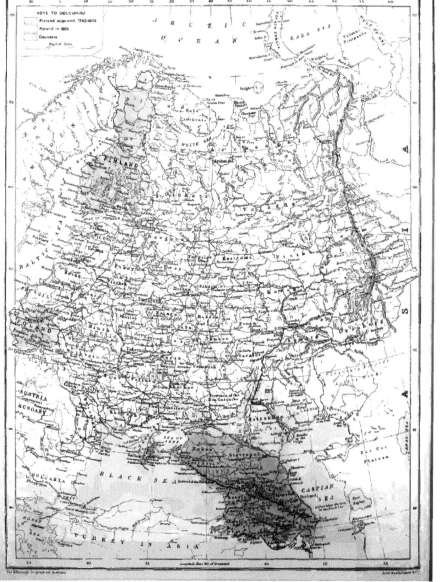

31

THE BALTIC

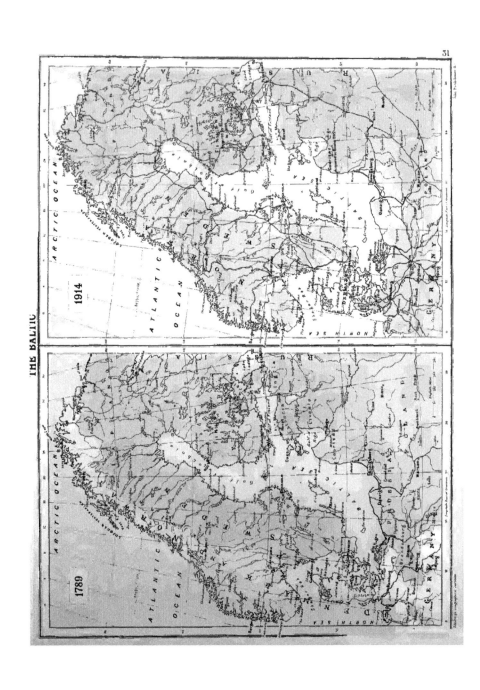

1789

1914

RUSSIA IN CENTRAL ASIA

PERSIA AND THE PERSIAN GULF, 1914

THE FAR EAST, 1914

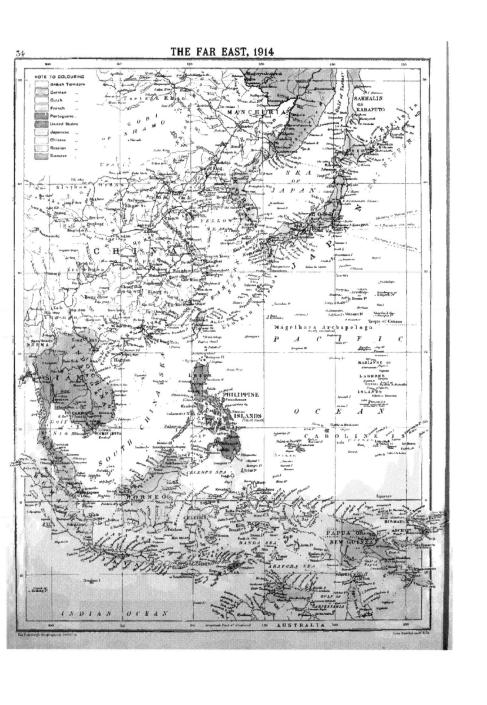

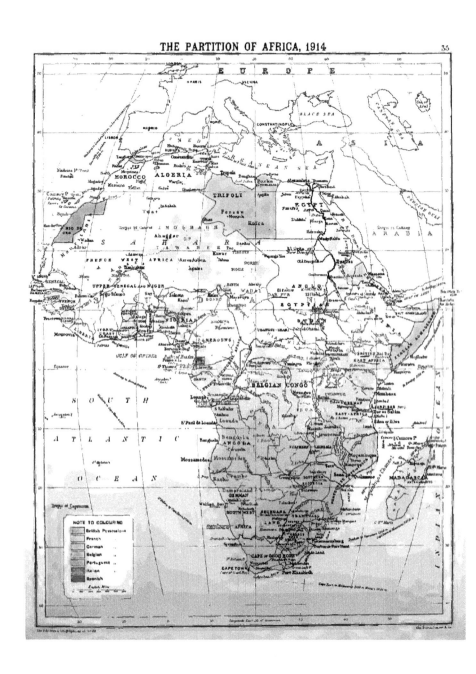

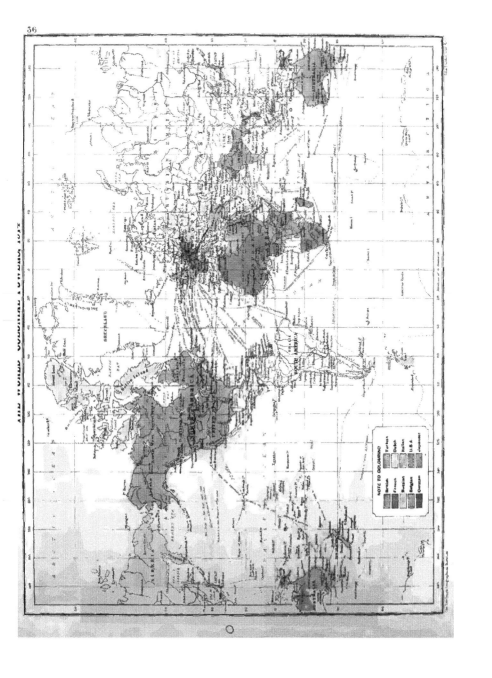